Providing Safe & Healthy WORKPLACE WITH ISO 45001:2018

IMPLEMENTATION OF OHSMS

RAMESH C GROVER
SACHIN GROVER

INDIA • SINGAPORE • MALAYSIA

Notion Press

Old No. 38, New No. 6
McNichols Road, Chetpet
Chennai - 600 031

First Published by Notion Press 2019
Copyright © Ramesh C Grover, Sachin Grover 2019
All Rights Reserved.

ISBN 978-1-64587-708-0

This book has been published with all efforts taken to make the material error-free after the consent of the author. However, the author and the publisher do not assume and hereby disclaim any liability to any party for any loss, damage, or disruption caused by errors or omissions, whether such errors or omissions result from negligence, accident, or any other cause.

While every effort has been made to avoid any mistake or omission, this publication is being sold on the condition and understanding that neither the author nor the publishers or printers would be liable in any manner to any person by reason of any mistake or omission in this publication or for any action taken or omitted to be taken or advice rendered or accepted on the basis of this work. For any defect in printing or binding the publishers will be liable only to replace the defective copy by another copy of this work then available.

Contents

Who Can Benefit From This Book?................. v
Foreword vii

1. Introduction 1
2. Need for ISO 45001 Standard? 4
3. How ISO 45001 Enables Organizations to
   Put an OH&S Management System in Place?...6
4. What Does ISO 45001 Mean for
   Users of OHSAS 18001?...................... 8
5. New/Updated Concepts in ISO 45001:2018 9
6. Why Adopt an Occupational Health and
   Safety Management System Standard?....... 21
7. Overview of New and Updated Concepts
   in ISO 45001:2018 22
8. What are the Benefits of ISO 45001:2018? 24
9. Gap Analysis 25
10. A Brief Clause Wise Overview of ISO
    45001:2018 Requirements Vis a Vis OHSAS
    18001:2007 – OH&S Management System 28

Conclusion..193
Bibliography 195
Correspondence Between
  ISO 45001:2018 and OHSAS 18001:2007 197

Contents

About Authors *203*
This Book Contains Expert Advice on
    How to Prepare for ISO 45001:2018,
       Implementation and Auditing................*205*

Who Can Benefit From This Book?

The guidelines given in this book are intended to assist organizations to develop and implement an effective OH&S Management System that can be integrated with other management systems. The implementation of an effective OH&S Management System is crucial for an organization to achieve a sound OH&S performance and comply with legal requirements and other obligations. Organizations of all types and sizes may use this guideline as it provides generic assistance for establishing, implementing and improving an OH&S Management System.

This book will benefit:

1. **Organizations preparing for ISO implementation:** This book is written primarily for those with moderate or no knowledge about ISO 45001 implementation
2. **ISO 45001 consultants:** This book gives guidelines to consultants, on how to prepare for ISO 45001:2018 implementations in the most logical way, with practical examples, helping you to look knowledgeable and helpful before your clients.

3. **Organizations planning updation of OHSAS 18001:2007:** Senior managers, engineers, executives, or project managers who have been given the responsibility for updation of OHSAS 18001 to ISO 45001:2018 standard in the organization, whatever be its size.

4. **Auditors (External/Internal):** This book will help Certification Body Auditors as well as Internal Auditors in better understanding of "what to look for" during the audit. This will ensure clear understanding of the requirements of the standard and thus avoid unnecessary arguments between auditors and auditees.

Foreword

Every year, millions of workers are injured or lose their lives globally from work-related accidents and diseases. Organizations worldwide recognize the need to provide a safe and healthy working environment, reduce the likelihood of accidents and demonstrate that they are actively managing risks. The new international standard for occupational health and safety, ISO 45001, will provide an internationally accepted framework that will help protect employees and in turn promote the health of an organization.

Daily across the globe, horrific statistics of health and safety incidents or accidents and their related costs are recorded. I was in a conference on agriculture couple of years back and was surprised to hear that in India, agriculture is the 2nd most accident prone profession backed by compelling data.

Although organizations tend to use generic health and safety guidelines or national and consortia standards or local regulations, none of these demonstrate global conformity based on a systems approach. There was a worldwide need to harmonize health and safety management systems using an international standard and sharing best practices.

This can be seen at local, national, regional and global levels – applying to both developing and developed countries. With an international standard to refer to, together with the right infrastructure and training, organizations will be able to address these risks better in future besides managing compliance to applicable regulations.

ISO 45001 brings occupational health and safety management and continual improvement into the heart of an organization. This new standard is an opportunity for organizations to align their strategic direction with their OH&S management system. In addition, there is an increased focus on improving occupational health and safety performance and culture.

This book provides an overview of the key changes between the OHSAS BS 18001:2007 and the ISO 45001:2018. You will need to prepare for change and adapt your OH&S management system to meet the new requirements.

The OH&S management system standard helps organisations manage their OH&S issues and to make efforts to reduce their impacts. In the past, organizations have adopted these practices to varying degrees and some organizations have used the standard in a minimal manner, just hang a Certificate on the wall or to satisfy tender requirements.

Why does this happen one wonders if OH&S is such an important subject? One fact is that we still do not understand how to understand and use the standard to help us define what good OHS system looks like.

While the pursuit of only a certificate is not the best approach to benefit from the distilled knowledge an international standard contains, sadly the Indian market has any number of unauthentic ISO certificates floating around and therefore, it is important to obtain an authentic certificate – which means an accredited certificate with international equivalence.

Ramesh and Sachin, the authors of this book, are vastly experienced and have written this book to bring all their experiences on paper and share them with a wider audience. Their effort is to help implement these practices holistically with the right support and attention from leadership, something that is lacking in many organizations, to reduce their impacts on the workers. They have tried to bring about a more complete understanding of the context the organization operates in. They have used examples that explain with common sense how we must do what we have to do, but more importantly help people understand why we do what we do to reduce our Hazards and Risks.

The international standards typically tell us what is needed to be done – they do not tell us how to do. This book tells us how to do what ISO 45001 requires us to do. And it gives us the insights that can only come from the vast experience collected by the authors over decades of working closely with businesses and helping them understand and implement the OHS. I am happy to recommend this book to anyone trying to implement the OHS practices correctly and hope it brings a change that will help their efforts to reduce OH&S impacts.

Anil Jauhri
CEO
National Accreditation Board for
Certification Bodies (NABCB)
C/o Quality Council of India
2nd Floor, Institution of Engineers Building,
2, Bahadur Shah Zafar Marg,
New Delhi – 110002
India

Introduction

According to the ILO estimates, every year over 2.78 million women and men die at work from an occupational injury or disease. Over 350,000 deaths are due to fatal accidents and almost 2 million deaths are due to fatal work-related diseases. In addition, over 313 million workers are involved in non-fatal occupational accidents causing serious injuries and absences from work. The ILO also estimates that 160 million cases of non-fatal work-related diseases occur annually. These estimates imply that every day approximately 7,800 people die from occupational accidents or diseases and that 860,000 people are injured on the job. Furthermore, as estimates show, work-related diseases represent the main cause of death at work, killing almost six times more workers than occupational accidents. The burden to employers and employees alike is immense, resulting in losses to the wider economy from staff absence and rising insurance premiums.

ISO 45001 is an international standard for occupational health and safety (OH&S), providing a framework for managing the prevention of death, work-related injury and ill health, with the aim of improving and providing a safe and healthy workplace for workers under the control of organization. The standard is intended to help organizations, regardless of size or industry, in designing systems to proactively prevent injury and ill health. All of its requirements are designed to be integrated into an organization's management processes.

The impact of Industrial activities on the Health & Safety of personnel is forcing the organizations to identify the hazards of their activities, products and services, assess the risk and determine controls for mitigating the health and safety risk. The ISO 45001 standard is primarily concerned with "Occupational Health and Safety management".

This means that the organization needs to:

- Identify the health and safety hazards of their activities, and plan to reduce the risk.
- achieve continual improvement in its OH&S management system and OH&S performance.

An Organization needs to understand the hazards of its activities, not just managing its Hazards, but taking action to manage those hazards that are directly impacting the organization and the health and safety of various interested parties. For this, the organizations need to have a well built OH&S management system leading to continual improvement.

An organization's activities can pose a risk of injury or ill-health, and can result in a serious impairment of health, or even fatality, to those working for or on its behalf; consequently, it is important for the organization to eliminate or minimize its OH&S risks by taking appropriate preventive measures. An organization's OH&S management system can help to prevent incidents through systematic and ongoing set of processes and can reinforce the organization's commitment to continually improving its OH&S performance.

This book has been designed to help organizations in understanding and meeting the requirements of the International Standard, ISO 45001:2018 **for its Implementation**, and for auditors to understand **what to look for** during verification of the compliance to ISO 45001:2018 requirements.

Need for ISO 45001 Standard?

This ISO 45001 standard helps the organizations to improve their health and safety performance by creating a secure work environment where injuries and illness are prevented.

ISO 45001, *Occupational health and safety management systems – Requirements with guidance for use*, provides the requirements for implementation of a management system and framework that reduces the risk of harm and ill health to employees.

Work-related stress is a significant societal issue. Greater expectations, increased competition and rapid changes in technology place pressure on employees to work harder and longer. This type of stress can result in to serious consequences towards health and well-being of personnel and the entire eco-system around them.

There is a lot that the organization can do to prevent and manage such stress, including effective well-being programmes and reducing any risks to health and safety that may occur as a result of their work.

Organizations around the world recognize the need to provide a safe and healthy environment so as to reduce the likelihood of any accidents. This will also help in demonstrating that the organization is actively managing the risks. ISO 45001 provides a framework that helps to protect employees from accidents. The standard is flexible and can be adapted to manage occupational health and safety in a wide range of organizations.

Like ISO 9001:2015 and ISO 14001:2015, ISO 45001:2018 is also based on the International Organization for Standardization's high level structure (HLS) for management system standards so implementing this standard will also help in integrating the requirements of ISO 45001 with other standards

How ISO 45001 Enables Organizations to Put an OH&S Management System in Place?

To survive, the Organizations need to ensure that they manage all their past incidents and potential health & safety risks. OH&S is an aspect, which every organization has to manage proactively. Apart from the impact on people, poor OH&S management can have many negative effects on organization, such as loss of competent staff, business disturbances, accident claims, higher insurance premiums, penalties from authorities, company image concerns, and, ultimately, the loss of business.

The standard follows the Plan-Do-Check-Act (PDCA) model, which provides a framework for organizations to plan what they need to do, in order to minimize the risk of harm. The measures should address those concerns that lead to long-term health issues for workers and their absence from work, as well as those that give rise to accidents. For example, many suffer from psychosocial tension (i.e. stress), which is believed to be one of the critical problems of the modern business and, apart from the misery caused to workers and their families, is a huge loss to society.

The standard requires that the top management should take accountability and demonstrate commitment to ensure that workers have the appropriate skills and that required controls are identified and put in place for implementation. The standard recognizes the worker participation & consultation to develop and apply improved OH&S practices.

What Does ISO 45001 Mean for Users of OHSAS 18001?

The standard, ISO 45001 helps organizations in improving OH&S performance through more efficient use of resources and reduction of incidents, preparation for controlling emergency situations and enhancing image of the company. In OHSAS 18001, there were certain requirements though Implied but now have been explicitly defined in the standard, like a plan for Communication in the form of a Communication Matrix.

ISO 45001 includes the need for **continual improvement** of an organization's systems and approach to OH&S concerns. The standard ISO 45001, ensures increased prominence of OH&S management within the organization's processes, with commitment from management for proactive initiatives that enhance OH&S performance.

New/Updated Concepts in ISO 45001:2018

Cl. 4   Context of the Organization

- Context is defined as the purpose that the organization is attempting to achieve and the external and internal issues that will impact the ability to achieve the intended outcome.

Provides a greater understanding of the important issues that can affect, positively or negatively the way the organization manages its OH&S goals.

Cl. 4.1   Understanding the Organization and Its Context

- Understand & determine issues (positive & negative) that can affect the ability of the organization to achieve its intended outcomes
- Issues include: conditions, characteristics or changing circumstances that can affect OH&S.

Cl. 4.2   Needs and Expectations of Workers and Other Interested Parties

Consider who are the interested parties and what their relevant interests might be, e.g. workers, customers, shareholders, board members, competitors and regulators. Consider the needs and expectations of interested parties that are relevant to your OH&S, then decide whether those needs and expectations need to be chosen for addressing within your OH&S system.

Needs & expectations of

- Both managerial & non-managerial workers & their representatives
- Legal & Regulatory authorities
- Parent Organization
- Suppliers, co-contractors & subcontractors
- Owners, shareholders, clients, visitors, local community, neighbours, general public

Note – When the organization chooses to adopt the Needs & expectations from interested parties they become obligatory requirements for the organization.

Cl. 4.3 Scope

When determining the scope, the organisation will consider:

a. The external and internal issues referred to in Cl.4.1;
b. Requirements referred to in Cl.4.2;
c. The work-related activities performed by the organization.

The organization shall review identified issues as per Cl.4.1 and Needs and Expectations of Interested parties as per Cl.4.2 and work-related activities to determine the Scope.

Cl. 5 Leadership and Worker Participation

Requirements specific to top management for demonstrating commitment and promoting a positive culture for occupational health & safety. The emphasis has shifted from 'ensuring' to "engaging" with workers through their consultation and participation in safety issues to improve performance, and to take overall responsibility and accountability for the prevention of work related injury and ill health.

Cl. 5.1   Leadership and Commitment

- Ensuring OH&S policy & objectives are established and are compatible with organizations strategic direction

- Integrating OH&S into organizational business processes

- Providing resources

- Ensuring active participation of workers & their representatives

- Ensuring that the OH&S management systems achieves intended outcome(s)

- Ensuring Continual Improvement of OH&S
- Supporting relevant management roles to demonstrate their leadership as it applies to their areas of responsibility
- Promoting a culture in organization that supports OH&S management system

Cl. 5.2 OH&S Policy

In the OH&S Policy, commitment to the communication and participation of workers, and commitment to provide safe and healthy working conditions also need to be defined.

Cl. 5.3 Organizational Roles, Responsibility and Authority

Top management shall ensure that the responsibilities and authorities for relevant roles within the OH&S management system are assigned and communicated at all levels within the organization and maintained as documented information. Workers at each level of the organization shall assume responsibility for those aspects of the OH&S management system over which they have control.

NOTE: While responsibility and authority can be assigned, ultimately top management is still accountable for the functioning of the OH&S management system.

Cl. 5.4 Participation and Consultation

To promote worker participation, and consultation and provide documented information to define their roles and responsibilities.

Cl. 6.1 Actions to Address Risks and Opportunities

When planning for the OH&S management system, the organization shall consider the issues referred to in Cl. 4.1 (Internal and external issues), the requirements referred to in Cl. 4.2 (Needs and Expectations of interested parties) and Cl. 4.3 (the scope of its OH&S management system) and determine the risks and opportunities that need to be addressed to:

a. give assurance that the OH&S management system can achieve its intended outcome(s);

b. prevent, or reduce, undesired effects;

c. achieve continual improvement.

Includes risks and opportunities OH&S risks & OH&S opportunities from the operations of the organization as well as those relating to the management system, mentioned as "Other Risk" and "Other Opportunities".

Cl. 6.1.2 Hazard identification and assessment of risks and opportunities

Cl. 6.1.2.1 Hazard Identification

Hazard identification should proactively identify any sources or situation arising from organizations activities, with potential for work-related injury & ill health. Sources/situations could include, but not limited to physical, chemical, biological, psychosocial, physiological; or mechanical and electrical

The process(es) shall take into account, but not be limited to:

- how work is organized, social factors (including workload, work hours, victimization, harassment and bullying), leadership and the culture in the organization;

Cl. 6.1.2.2 Assessment of OH&S risks and other risks to the OH&S management system

The organization shall establish, implement and maintain process(es) to:

a. assess OH&S risks from the identified hazards, while taking into account the effectiveness of existing controls;

b. determine and assess the other risks related to the establishment, implementation, operation and maintenance of the OH&S management system.

Cl. 6.1.2.3 Assessment of OH&S opportunities and other opportunities for the OH&S management system

The organization shall establish, implement and maintain process(es) to assess:

a. OH&S opportunities to enhance OH&S performance, while taking into account planned changes to the organization, its policies, its processes or its activities and:

   1. opportunities to adapt work, work organization and work environment to workers;

   2. opportunities to eliminate hazards and reduce OH&S risks;

b. other opportunities for improving the OH&S management system.

Cl. 6.2 OH&S Objectives and Planning to Achieve Them

Objectives must support the Strategic direction and policy requirements and should have been considered in line with available resources.

Action plans to achieve Objectives

There should be plan detailing:

1. What will be done?
2. What resources will be required?
3. Who will be responsible?
4. When it will be completed?
5. How it will be measured through indicators (if practicable) & monitored?
6. How results will be evaluated?

Cl. 7.1 Resources

Examples of resources include human, natural, infrastructure, technology and financial.

Examples of infrastructure include the organization's buildings, plant, equipment, utilities, information technology and communications systems, and emergency containment systems.

Cl. 7.2 Competence

Includes competence on ability to identify hazards

Cl. 7.3 Awareness

Where workers identify potential for danger or a hazardous OH&S which can cause injury and/or ill health, they should be able to remove themselves &

inform the organization of the circumstances without risk of penalization.

Cl. 7.4 Communication

The new clause now strengthens the previous requirements: objective of the communication and its effectiveness

Cl. 7.5 Documented Information

Replaces documents and records in OHSAS 18001

- Organization will need to maintain & retain documentation information of OH&S objectives & plans to achieve them, keeping complexity to minimum
- Aimed at preventing the risk of unintended use of obsolete documented information

Cl. 8.1 Operational Planning and Control

More detailed requirements in relation to multi-employer workplaces, hierarchy of controls, management of change, outsourcing, procurement and contractors have been added.

Cl. 8.1.2 Eliminating hazards and reducing OH&S risks

The organization shall establish, implement and maintain a process(es) for the elimination of hazards and reduction of OH&S risks using the following hierarchy of controls

Cl. 8.1.3 Management of Change

Requirement to consider the planned changes of the operation e.g. working conditions, equipment, workforce and changes to legal requirements and known hazards and risks and plan for the requirements for the management of hese changes.

Cl. 8.1.4 Procurement

Establish controls to ensure that the procurement of goods (for example products, hazardous materials or substances, raw materials, equipment) and services conform to its OH&S management system requirements.

Prior to procuring goods & services, the organization should identify procurement controls that:

- Identify & evaluate potential OH&S risks associated with products, materials, equipment, service
- Requirements for products, materials, equipment, services to conform to OH&S objectives

- Need for information, participation & communications
- Before being released for use by workers verify equipment, installations & materials are adequate

Cl. 8.1.4.2 Contractors

The establishment of controls required with regard to contractor's work, the host company's work activities, consideration shall be given to competence and safety requirements for contractor workers in relation to OH&S criteria.

Cl. 8.1.4.3 Outsourced Processes

Organization shall ensure that **outsourced processes** affecting OH&S management system are controlled.

Cl. 9.1 Performance Evaluation

Measurement of operations that can have an impact on legal requirements, operational controls, OH&S risks, opportunities & OH&S performance

Cl. 9.2 Internal Audit

The extent of the audit programme should be based on the complexity and level of maturity of the OH&S management system.

Cl. 9.3 Management Review

More detailed requirements relating to inputs and outputs of the review

Cl. 10 Improvement

The organization should consider the results from analysis and evaluation of OH&S performance, evaluation of compliance, internal audits and management review when taking action to improve.

Examples of improvement include corrective action, continual improvement, breakthrough change, innovation and re-organization.

Cl. 10.2 Incident, Non Conformity and Corrective Action

Root cause analysis is the key to progressive improvement and requires the organisation to determine what caused the incident or nonconformity, what needs to be done to address the cause, review any risk assessments or establish a new assessment, where required before implementing an action.

More detailed process requirements and no need of preventive action due to risk based approach.

Why Adopt an Occupational Health and Safety Management System Standard?

ISO 45001 is the business improvement tool that helps organizations in analysing their activities proactively and systematically for their Occupational Health & Safety hazards that may lead to a Significant risk and once potential significant Hazards are identified, decide the controls required to avoid or reduce the impact of the hazard by either reducing the severity or minimising the probability of occurrence of the hazard.

Overview of New and Updated Concepts in ISO 45001:2018

ISO 45001 is based on Annex SL – the new ISO high level structure (HLS) that brings a common framework to all management systems. The Plan-Do-Check-Act (PDCA) cycle is applicable to all processes and to the OH&S management system as a whole. The diagram (Figure 1) illustrates how Clauses 4 to 10 are interlinked in relation to PDCA. High Level Structure helps keep consistency, align different management system standards, and apply common language across all standards. It makes it easier for organizations to incorporate their OH&S management system, into core business processes, with more involvement from senior management.

- HLS also requires that organisation shall determine external and internal issues that are relevant to its purpose and that affect its ability to achieve intended outcome.

- This approach is intended to increase value of such standards to users, particularly those operating multiple Management Systems simultaneously contained within one System (Integrated Management System).

ISO 45001 is a standard that helps organizations in implementing the OH&S management system, making it more flexible and sustainable. It brings OH&S management into the culture of the organization, complementing business strategy and helps in improving OH&S performance. ISO 45001 is the standard that is a framework which helps the organizations to focus on the increasing expectations of customers, other interested parties, as well as regulatory agencies.

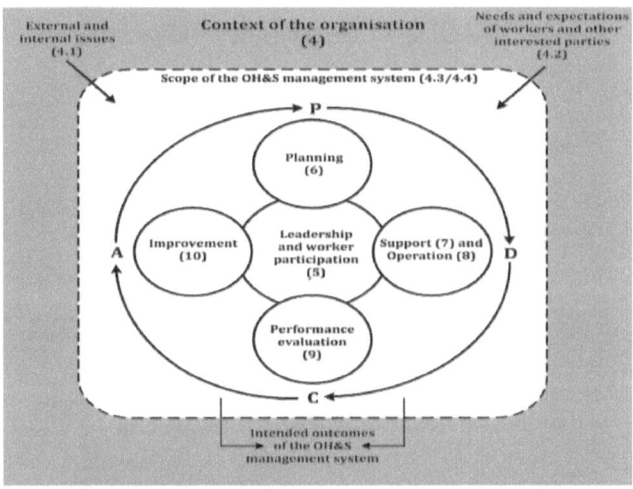

Relationship between PDCA and the framework in this document

The most important change in the standard is an opportunity for organizations to align their strategic planning with their OH&S management system. In addition, there is an increased focus on improving OH&S performance

What are the Benefits of ISO 45001:2018?

Implementing ISO 45001:2018 has many benefits for organizations, since using the standard helps them:

- Proactive and not Reactive Approach
- Understand needs and expectations of Interested parties
- Manage OH&S Compliance Obligations
- Culture of Continual Improvement in OH&S performance
- Protect the workers, including the prevention or reduction of injury and illness;
- Improve Communication with relevant interested parties.
- Increase new business opportunities
- Increase stakeholder and customer trust.

Gap Analysis

Do we need to carry out a Gap Analysis for ISO 45001:2018 implementation? Organizations already using OHSAS 18001:2007 are recommended to take the following actions:

i. Identify organizational gaps which need to be addressed to meet new requirements.

ii. Develop an implementation plan.

iii. Provide appropriate training and awareness to all concerned whose activities have an impact on the effectiveness of the organisation.

iv. Update the existing Occupational Health & Safety management system (OHSMS) to meet the revised requirements and provide verification of effectiveness.

The organizations, which have already been certified to OHSAS 18001, it is imperative that:

- They would be meeting legislative requirements,
- They would have evaluated the hazards & risks of their activities, products and services,

- They would have identified Objectives & Targets and made programs to achieve the objectives for continual improvement in their Occupational Health & Safety Management System.

Even otherwise, sometimes, it can be expected that an organization may already be undertaking some of the actions needed to satisfy parts of the ISO 45001 standard, even though they are not yet certified. Therefore, it is helpful to conduct a gap analysis to find the gap between the existing status and further requirements in terms of the ISO 45001:2018 standard, which may not be too wide.

How to carry out Gap Analysis?

To carry out a Gap analysis, the analysing team should,

- talk to key personnel who are knowledgeable about the internal processes within the organization. Examine the activities already being carried out vis a vis the ISO 45001:2018 requirements and use the gap analysis to find the difference between existing processes & documents and the standard's requirements

- review the Competence of the various level of personnel for the implementation of OHSMS in a way that ensures that the requirements of the ISO 45001:2018 standard can be met? If required, there may be a need to further train some key personnel to fill the gap.

- Review the Legal & other requirements applicable, particularly any new requirements and the status of implementation in the organization

This will provide an assessment of how the current OHSMS and its performance can be aligned with the ISO 45001:2018 requirements.

A Brief Clause Wise Overview of ISO 45001:2018 Requirements Vis a Vis OHSAS 18001:2007 – OH&S Management System

The ISO 45001:2018 version is based on HLS structure having ten main requirements as shown

High-Level Structure (HLS)

1. Scope
2. Normative Reference
3. Terms and Definitions
4. Context of the Organization
5. Leadership
6. Planning
7. Support
8. Operation
9. Performance Evaluation
10. Improvement

1. Scope

The standard ISO 45001 specifies requirements for an occupational health and safety (OH&S) management system, and gives guidance for its use, that help to provide safe and healthy workplaces by preventing work-related injury and ill health, as well as by proactively improving its OH&S performance.

This standard is useable by any organization regardless of its size, type and activities. It is applicable to the OH&S risks of the activities under the organization's control, taking into account factors such as the context in which the organization operates and the needs and expectations of its workers and other interested parties.

The standard does not address issues such as product safety, property damage or environmental impacts, beyond the risk to workers and other relevant interested parties.

2. Normative References

No normative references mentioned in the standard

3. Terms and Definitions

Broad categorization

- **Terms related to organization and leadership**
- **Terms related to planning**
- **Terms related to support and operation**
- **Terms related to performance evaluation and improvement**

Worker

- person performing work or work related activities that are under the control of the *organization*

Note: *worker refers to everyone working under the control of the organization, including business owners, managers, interns, volunteers, all employees and contractors.*

Participation

- involvement in decision making

Note: *participation relates to taking part in something, whilst in relation to the standard it means involvement in decision-making, e.g. jointly carrying out risk assessment and being involved in deciding the organization's OH&S policy and objectives.*

Consultation

- seeking views before making a decision

Workplace

- place under the control of the *organization*, where a person needs to be or to go for work purposes

Note: For the OH&S controls, the workplace depends on the degree of control over the area.

Contractor

- external *organization* providing services to the organization in accordance with agreed specifications, terms and conditions

Note: Terms and conditions to control the Occupational Health & Safety of all personnel based on the activities carried out by the contractors at site

Outsource

- make an arrangement where an external *organization* performs part of an organization's function or *process*

Note: An external organization is outside the scope of the *management system*, although the outsourced function or process is within the scope.

Incident

- *occurrence arising out of, or in the course of, work that could or does result in injury and ill health*

Objective

- *result to be achieved*

Objectives can be strategic, tactical or operational:

- *strategic objectives can be set to improve the overall performance of the OH&S management system (e.g. to eliminate noise exposure);*

- *tactical objectives can be set at facility, project or process level (e.g. to reduce noise at source);*
- *operational objectives can be set at the activity level (e.g. the enclosure of individual machines to reduce noise).*

Legal Requirements and Other Requirements

- *legal requirements that an organization has to comply with and other requirements that an organization has to or chooses to comply with*

Occupational Health and Safety Risk (OH&S Risk)

- *combination of the likelihood of occurrence of a work related hazardous event or exposure(s) and the severity of injury and ill health that can be caused by the event or exposure(s)*

Occupational Health and Safety Opportunity (OH&S Opportunity)

- *circumstance or set of circumstances that can lead to improvement of OH&S performance*

Occupational Health and Safety Performance (OH&S Performance)

- *performance related to the effectiveness of the prevention of injury and ill health to workers and the provision of safe and healthy workplaces*

Risk

- *Effect of Uncertainty*

Risk Assessment

Risk assessment is the process where you:

- *Identify hazards and risk factors that have the potential to cause harm (hazard identification).*
- *Analyze and evaluate the risk associated with that hazard (risk analysis, and risk evaluation).*
- *Determine appropriate ways to eliminate the hazard, or control the risk when the hazard cannot be eliminated (risk control).*

Hazard

- *Source with a potential to cause injury and ill health*

Hazards can include sources with the potential to cause harm or hazardous situations, or circumstances with the potential for exposure leading to injury and ill health.

4.0 Context of the Organization

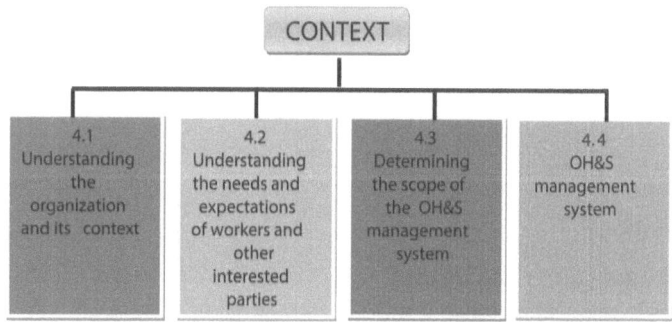

4.1 Understanding the Organization and Its Context

As per OHSAS 18001:2007, an organization was just considering the hazards of the activities, to identify their risk and actions were considered to reduce the organization's hazards.

This clause provides guidance on understanding what can affect an organization's ability to manage its OH&S responsibilities and achieve its intended outcomes.

The organization must understand the internal and external issues that can impact in a positive or negative manner on its health and safety performance including, internal and external issues such as cultural, social, political, legal, financial, technological, economic, market competition and natural factors of significance to its performance.

The company will be required to identify all relevant internal and external issues including conditions, characteristics or changing circumstances that can affect its occupational health and safety management system.

This clause requires identification of relevant external and internal issues that affect organization's ability to achieve the intended outcome(s) of its OH&S Management System. The intended outcomes include:

- Improving the organization's health and safety performance
- Meeting its compliance obligations
- Achieving its health and safety objectives

This also includes identifying interested parties, their needs and expectations, which will assist in determining the scope of the organization's management system and putting in place the processes needed to support it.

The term **"intended outcomes"** means the goals that the organization intends to achieve. For Example, enhancement of OH&S performance, fulfilment of its compliance obligations and reduction in number of incidents. Generally the intended outcome for an organization is to prevent injury and ill-health, to improve and enhance the safety and health of its workers and the other persons under its control.

An organization can set additional objectives, such as going beyond the OH&S management system or legislative requirements, for example by adopting social and OH&S sustainability principles, if it decides that it could benefit from this. As an example, if the Hazardous emissions are within the Legal norms, still the organization can plan to further reduce the emissions to meet their responsibility towards society for controlling the health impact. That becomes an opportunity for the organization for improvement in OH&S Performance. **ISO 45001** is a new international standard for occupational health and safety (OH&S), providing a framework for managing the prevention of death, work-related injury and ill health, with the intended outcome of improving and providing a safe and healthy workplace for workers and persons under an organization's control

The term 'issue' does not only cover problems, but also important topics for the OH&S Management System to address, such as any goals for achievement that the organization might set for itself under its OH&S Management System. Importantly, those issues should include not only working conditions but also those by which it gets affected. Eg a severe Air Quality Index (AQI) in the region will force the organization to control the emissions of dust and gasses (such as PM 10, PM 2.5, SOx, NOx, CO, NH_3 and Ozone that increase the AQI level. It is important to understand the influencing factors for the organization, to make a fact based risk evaluation and to build a management system that is efficient and able to achieve intended outcomes.

The biggest challenge will be to understand and analyse external issues that have influence on the organization's activities from the OH&S perspective. The organization may need to review and evaluate appropriate information which can include various functions e.g. design, purchase, legal, Maintenance, HR as well as Production. The external context for an organization is dependent on several factors, such as business sector, size, geographical location, applicable legislations, competition etc.

The context of the organization can be classified as:

- **Internal context**: any organization's activity, products and services that may affect the organization's OH&S performance
- **External context**: which may include legal issues, economic, social, technical or political issues
- **Working conditions** means the hazards which may result in damage to the organization's OH&S performance,

Therefore, we can imagine the importance of having a good awareness of the context of our own organization to ensure that we not only meet OH&S objectives and expectations, but also have a foundation to ensure we are aware of satisfying all external interested parties and preparing for the future.

The company will be required to identify all relevant internal and external issues including conditions, characteristics or changing circumstances that can affect its occupational health and safety management system and then address those that require further attention.

External issues include the following:

- The cultural, social, political, legal, financial, technological and economic conditions in which the company operates, whether at international, national, regional or local level;
- The legislative framework in which the organization operates including statutory, regulatory and other forms of legal requirements;
- Competition and market conditions;
- Relationship with contractors, suppliers, partners and other external interested parties;

- Key drivers and trends of relevance to the industry or sector in which the organization operates.

Internal issues include the following:

- The strategic direction of the organization, its policies and objectives;
- Organizational governance and structure, roles and accountabilities;
- The capability and capacity of the organization in terms of resources, knowledge and competence (e.g. capital, employee competencies, processes, systems and technologies);
- Health and safety culture of the organization;
- Relationship with Contractors;
- Working time arrangements;
- Working conditions;

An understanding of the organization and its context can be achieved at a strategic level by using techniques such as Strengths, Weaknesses, Opportunities and Threats (SWOT) analysis. Alternatively, brainstorming may be done to identify the issues.

Implementing an OH&S management system is a strategic decision influenced by the 'context of the organisation', which means identification of the internal and external issues relevant to your organisation.

Internal issues	External issues
Governance, structure, roles and accountabilities	Economic factors (e.g. exchange rates, economic situation, inflation, availability of credit)
Policies, objectives, strategies	Market factors (e.g. competition, trends in customer growth, market stability, supply chain relationships)
Introduction of new products, software, tools, premises and equipment	Technological factors (e.g. new technology, materials and equipment, patents expiring)
Company culture	
Working time arrangements etc.	

To understand which issues are important, an organization should consider those that:

- are key drivers and trends
- can present problems
- reflect changing circumstances
- can be leveraged for beneficial effect, including improved OH&S performance
- present opportunities for competitive advantage, including cost reduction, value for customers, or
- improvement of the organization's reputation and "brand".

Examples of internal issue:

1. A company operates a chemical plant. There is only one person in the plant having knowledge of critical plant operations. If he suddenly leaves the company, the new person who may not have enough knowledge of the operation will have higher probability of the hazard and so the organization needs to plan for a controlled "transfer" of his knowledge to ensure continuity of the operations in a safe manner.

2. A house hold goods manufacturing company is facing issues related to depreciation of assets related to safety e.g. tools and tackles. Hence, the company needs to address the issues related to the up gradation of the assets with respect to safety.

3. A supplier for an electronic component was forced to make their workers work over time due to the supply pressure during holiday seasons.

4. The workers of a company were frequently facing incidents due to poor quality of the personnel protective equipment but there is no system or forum for grievance redressal in company.

5. A Company was facing repeated issues in the event of fire incidents due to hold up of budget by the top management for installation of Carbon dioxide based fire-extinguishing system.

6. A company was not carrying out investigation for the safety incidents it faced due to introduction of new software for management and reporting of incidents. The employees were not aware about the software capabilities.

7. Strikes were carried out by the workers in an auto parts manufacturing company for wrongful discharge or dismissal of workers due to a safety incident.

8. There were problems reported in handling of containers since the workers were not provided training on Safe handling of hydra in a company that operates port.

9. The road safety standards, guidelines and policies were not updated by a logistics company leading to many safety incidents.

10. Workers were not giving proper response to the top management of an Auto manufacturer due to lack in trust when the top management asked feedback on vibration and noise issues in the plant.

11. The Managing director of a company chose not to follow the advice of his health and safety adviser and instead adopted an attitude, allowing the standards in his business to fall leading

to governance failure and increase in safety incidents.

12. Frequent incidents were occurring in an oil Refinery plant since workers were unaware about the process safety requirements.

13. Due to poor ventilation the smoke was accumulated inside a moulding company causing ill health to the workers and the company was not even monitoring the pollution and health levels.

14. There was huge accumulation of fumes generated due to the welding in an automotive parts manufacturing plant because of the change in layout carried out but the ventilation system was not modified according to the change in layout.

Examples of external issues:

1. (Potential threat): A Cement plant is dependent on the coal being extracted from a mine nearby. The quality of coal is very good, with low Sulphur and high GCV but after a few years they need to source coal from another mine which will have high traces of Sulphur than the ore used today. This may be a possible threat in relation to their OH&S permit as their emissions to air may exceed the limits. The company will have to plan for the addition of another equipment and/or process to stay within the limits.

2. (Potential opportunity): An organization is manufacturing and marketing gas recovery equipment to avoid emissions of VOCs to air. New regulations will require for ship owners to install Gas recovery units for loading/unloading of fuel. This is a big potential new market for the organization and may plan to be ready to meet the market needs.

3. A chemical industry is increasingly faced with social pressure related to their use of a hazardous chemical. Competitors are switching to alternate chemical so the sales of this company are getting affected.

4. There are several changes brought to the safety norms by the national body that sets up automotive industry standards, Hence Automotive industries have to address such changes to meet the requirements of country specific National standards.

5. A company that operates and maintains Thermal power plant on behalf of the client has faced challenges due to their shared safety responsibilities such a scheduling meetings on Safety, analysis of incidents, reporting on safety performance and control on contractors. The Company need to address such shared safety responsibilities.

6. Half of the workers working in a textile company were hired on monthly basis. To make the new workers aware of the companies' safety requirements and hazards was becoming difficult for the Human Resource Department.

7. Desired number of people were not available due to shortage of workers in a construction company. Workers were made to frequently interchange their roles and responsibilities like working at height.

8. A company was carrying out expansion of their existing facility and had hired an external construction firm to carry out the project. Safety Incidents occurred frequently because the external firm had no system adopted for the management of safety. There was no system for verification of safety system adopted by external agency during the contractor selection phase

9. Safety Incidents occur in the gas pipeline industry due to lack of knowledge of the product (gas) and its hazard by the persons living in the nearby area.

10. An Automotive supplier was not able to implement customer specific requirements related environment i.e. guidelines related to restriction of hazardous substances due to lack of in-house testing facilities

The clause also talks about "OH&S conditions being affected by or capable of affecting the organization."

What should the organization do?

- Knowledge of internal and external issues and conditions is key input to the determination of risks and opportunities. Involvement of top management in identifying the issues based on organizational context.

Considerations for determining the Internal & External issues could include:

- To gain a comprehensive understanding of the organizational context, discuss with the top management to understand the strategic perspectives.

- This will help to understand the Internal and External issues with due consideration of what the strategies of the organization are with respect to the OH&S. Eg. Company's strategic direction is to reduce Volatile Organic Compounds (VOC) emissions so the organization shall make an objective to meet this strategic direction of the company.

External Issues:

Political: type of political system in place, e.g. Political interference in business development, willingness of politicians to exercise power effectively;

Economic: availability of resources, such as fuel, gas and water, infrastructure and transportation;

Competition: Concepts that can be adopted to maintain a competitive position when necessary, such as sustainability;

Technological: availability and access to technology relevant to the organization; e.g. new technology, materials and equipment

Legal: the legislative framework within which the organization operates;

Internal Issues:

The strategic direction of the organization, its policies and Objectives:

Does the Strategic direction clearly define the OH&S goals of the organization and are the Policies and Objectives related to the Strategic direction?

Company Culture: Does the organization consider OH&S as a value similar to the value they consider for Productivity & Quality of Product

Governance, Roles and Accountabilities: Has the Leadership clearly defined the roles, responsibilities and accountabilities for controlling the OH&S issues

These Internal and External issues that may hinder the achievement of Intended Outcomes, may change over time So identification of these issues has to be a recurring process to reflect changes in the external and internal issues.

Apart from this, the organization must understand the processes for the organizational context. For this, speak with mid-level managers within the organizational context to obtain their opinions, ideas, and challenges. Also observe workers performing the actual tasks; speak with those doing the work to understand their issues.

What the Auditors should look for:

- Context of the Organization is the first auditable part of ISO 45001:2018 and may be audited toward the beginning of the OH&S audit.

- Auditors will check how the internal and external issues are systematically summarized and presented so as to use it in an effective way? The changes to these issues shall also be audited periodically to ensure risk mitigation.

- Determine internal and external issues and conditions

For example:

1. who are involved?
2. what are their sources of information?
3. how is the information presented/used within the organisation?

Evidence of proper review may be through minutes of meetings, SWOT analysis, strategic analyses of market situation, etc.

4.2 Understanding the Needs and expectations of Workers and Other Interested Parties

- Determine Relevant interested parties,
- Determine needs and expectations of interested parties which are relevant to OH&S requirements.

This Clause requires identification of the interested parties for your OH&S Management System and understanding of the needs and expectations of those interested parties and determine the relevant needs and expectations of these parties so that you can determine which of these needs and expectations become compliance obligations.

ISO 45001 requires the organization to determine:

- The other interested parties, in addition to workers, that are relevant to the OH&S management system

- The relevant needs and expectations or requirements of workers and other interested parties

- Which of these needs and expectations are or could become legal and/or other requirements?

We need to understand the requirements of interested parties, the OH&S Management System Scope and OH&S Policy must be made available to them, and management needs to review any communication from external interested parties.

This Clause also deals with making the scope of the OH&S Management System and the OH&S Policy available to interested parties, and requires that management review includes an appraisal of any communications from external interested parties.

Different people and organizations are interested in your OH&S Management System for various reasons, and thinking about this when you are identifying the interested parties and determining their needs and expectations can be helpful. Below is a list of interested parties which have an interest in the performance of your OH&S Management System:

- **Workers/Contractor Employees**: Workers constitute the organization's most significant interested party, whose needs and expectations must be identified and addressed. The organization should seek out their views on health and safety concerns regarding work activities, products or services. It should follow up on inquiries, requests, complaints or suggestions made by workers to learn more about their expectations. Expectations of Employees/Contractor employees are to work in a safe and healthy environment, and they also wish to contribute to the improvement of the OH&S performance and OH&S Management System. The health and safety committee is an excellent forum for the gathering and evaluation of workers' concerns.

- **Management:** The management of your organization would want you to follow safety culture so that there is no injury or ill health due to company operations.

- **Community:** If your activities have the potential to cause hazards in the neighbourhood, such as gaseous emissions or noise, then your neighbours will want you to control your OH&S Management System.

- **Shareholders:** Shareholders of your company want you to make money and not waste it, which is why they agreed to implement an OH&S Management System in the first place. They will be interested in your OH&S Management System for the ability you have to meet requirements and avoid penalties.

- **Customers**: Your customers do not want you to impact the delivery of your product due to a penalty by legal authorities. They may also have OH&S targets of their own that can be more easily met with your involvement, such as a target to reduce number of near misses.

- **Regulatory Authorities**: No matter where you have your business, there will be regulations that need to be met. This is particularly true of OH&S regulations. Not meeting the Statutory requirements can mean fines or other penalties.

It is also important to note that the organization's stakeholder expectations may change over time, therefore a continual review of the needs and expectations of interested parties is required.

The expectations of interested parties may include legal and mandatory requirements and also investor/lender expectations, customer expectations, expectations of the local community, society as a whole and so on. It is required to document the needs and expectations of the interested parties, in order to ensure you can recognize and measure against the objectives you have set.

An organization can set additional objectives, such as going beyond the OH&S management system or legislative requirements, for example by adopting social and OH&S sustainability principles, if it feels that it could benefit from this. As an example, if the Hazardous emissions are within the Legal norms, still the organization can plan to further reduce the emissions to meet their responsibility towards society for controlling the health impact. That becomes an opportunity for the organization for improvement in OH&S Performance. **ISO 45001** providing a framework for managing the prevention of death, work-related injury and ill health, with the intended outcome of improving and providing a safe and healthy workplace for workers and persons under an organization's control

What the Organization should do?

One of the ways to identify your Compliance Obligations is:

- Ask your workers to identify the risks involved in their work areas and the opportunities for improvement in their OH&S performance. This can also be used as a record of Consultation with the workers.

Worker Name	Department	Activity	Risk	Opportunity
		e.g. Material movement		
		Welding		
		Machining		
		Transportation		
		Rigging		
		Piling		
		Any other		

- Ensure that you identify your Compliance obligations, working toward meeting those requirements, and keeping up to date on any changes in requirements. Without using a process to identify the interested parties and their needs and expectations, it is difficult to ensure that you have identified all the requirements you should address. Having identified the needs and expectations of interested parties, your management should review any comments they may have about your OH&S performance and decide action to satisfy the needs and expectations of the interested parties.

- An organization is expected to gain a general understanding of the expressed needs and expectations of those internal and external interested parties that have been determined to be relevant, so that the knowledge gained can be considered. The organization can then choose some of those needs and expectations for Compliance and would then be obliged to comply it. This way, from the needs and expectations of the interested parties, a compliance obligation is developed.

What the Auditors should look for?

- Has the organization identified the needs and expectations of their internal and external interested parties?

- While identifying the needs, has the organization considered its processes and OH&S issues that may affect the interested parties?

- Auditors need to understand the activities of the organization and discuss on their plans to meet the needs and expectations of interested parties.

- Whether the changes to the interested parties needs & expectations have an impact on the Organizations OH&S management system and are the controls in place.

4.3 Scope of the OHSMS

Review the scope and boundaries of the OH&S Management System considering the needs &

expectations of relevant interested parties, and resulting compliance obligations. Also requiring consideration, are the OH&S Management System functions and physical boundaries, and all products, services, and activities, including the organization's ability to control their activities.

Apart from activities, products and services, the following needs to be considered in defining the scope of OH&S Management System of your organization:

- External and internal issues identified in the "context of the organization": Both must be considered to ensure the scope is defined correctly and the OH&S Management System is effective. External factors may be the needs of neighbours, political factors, and so forth.

- Compliance Obligations: Obviously, all compliance obligations must be considered and met during implementation of your OH&S Management System.

- The organizational units, functions, and physical boundaries: This is self-explanatory, as these factors are part of the basic considerations in terms of how your organization actually operates.

What the Organization should do?

The scope shall be documented. It shall be established based on determination of the boundaries and applicability of the management system and by taking into consideration relevant inputs from Context and issues as well as needs and expectations of relevant interested parties.

Defining "Scope" is intended to clarify the boundaries of the organization to which the OH&S Management System will apply. Once the scope is defined, all activities, products and services of the organization within that scope need to be included in the OH&S Management System. Where a part of an organization is excluded from the scope of its OH&S Management System, the organization should be able to explain the exclusion.

What the Auditors should look for?

Scope should always be an important element for auditors to discuss and clarify with audited organization. Has the organization taken into consideration their contexts and issues and needs and expectations of the relevant interested parties in defining the Scope of implementation.

An organization has the freedom and flexibility to define its boundaries and may choose to implement an OH&S Management System with respect to the entire organization, or to specific operating units of the organization.

4.4 OH&S Management System

The standard ISO 45001:2018 requires that an OH&S Management System should be established to achieve the intended outcome by using interacting processes and using the information from contextual issues and "needs and expectations" of interested parties, to deliver continual improvement. The ultimate objective is to improve the organization's OH&S performance.

To establish an OH&S Management System, the organization needs to follow PDCA cycle as follows:

Plan:

1. understand the organization and its context, including the needs and expectations of workers and other interested parties
2. determine the scope of the OH&S management system
3. ensure leadership and commitment from top management
4. establish an OH&S policy
5. assign responsibilities and authorities for relevant roles

6. identify hazards and associated risks
7. identify and have access to compliance obligations
8. determine the OH&S risks and other risks
9. determine OH&S opportunities and other opportunities that need to be addressed
10. plan to take actions to address risks and opportunities determined, and evaluate effectiveness of these actions
11. establish OH&S objectives and define indicators and a programme to achieve them

Do:

1. determine the resources (manpower, skill and budget) required to implement and maintain the OH&S management system
2. establish, implement and maintain the processes needed for internal and external communications
3. ensure an appropriate method for creating and updating and controlling documented information
4. plan, implement and control operational controls needed to meet the OH&S management system requirements.

5. Define controls for eliminating hazards and reducing OH&S risks by following hierarchy of controls.

6. Manage the changes, Control procurement to ensure conformity to OH&S management system

7. Control OH&S risk arising from Contractual activities and functions and processes of Outsourced activities, thus ensuring that the requirements of management system are met

8. determine potential emergency situations and the response requirement

Check:

1. monitor, measure, analyse and evaluate OH&S performance and determine the effectiveness of the OH&S management system.

2. evaluate fulfilment of compliance obligations

3. conduct periodic internal audits to provide information that the OH&S management system is being effectively implemented

4. Carry out Management Review to know the organization's continuing suitability, adequacy and effectiveness OH&S management system

Act:

1. take action to deal with nonconformity by taking Corrective action based on the root cause analysis for the nonconformity.

2. take action to continually improve the suitability, adequacy and effectiveness of the OH&S management system to enhance OH&S performance

What the Auditors Should Look For?

- That the organization is working on enhancement of OH&S performance, fulfilment of compliance obligations and achievement of OH&S objectives. "Enhancing its OH&S performance" is a clear indication that the intent of an OH&S is to enhance the OH&S performance and improve continually its OH&S Management System.

- That the organization has also used the knowledge gained through contextual issues and "needs and expectations" of the interested parties in the process of enhancement of their OH&S performance.

- Whether root cause analysis is being done to identify the cause of non-conformity and Corrective action taken to avoid recurrence of the non-conformity.

5.0 Leadership

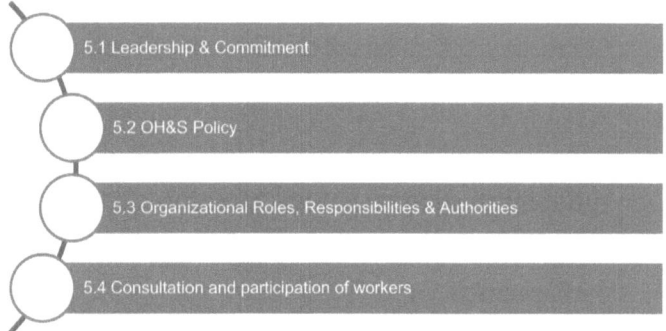

5.1 Leadership & Commitment

Top Management to ensure:

- **Policy and objectives are compatible with strategic direction**
- **Integration of the OH&S requirements into business processes**
- **OH&S policy is communicated, understood & applied**
- **Promotion of risk-based thinking**

This clause places accountability for implementing OH&S Management System on 'top management' which is the person or group of people who directs and controls the organization at the highest level. The purpose of these requirements is to demonstrate leadership and commitment by leading from the top and wherever possible integration of OH&S management into business processes.

Top Management involvement in ISO 45001 ensures the effective implementation of the OH&S management system as it makes the Top management Accountable and not just ***"Responsible"*** for an effective OH&S management system. Please note that Responsibility can be delegated but Accountability cannot be delegated, So top management may now delegate the responsibility for implementation of OH&S to others, but Accountability for the effective implementation of the OH&S lies with the top management only.

This includes commitment of Top management specific to an organization's context beyond those directly doing their assigned jobs. An important requirement now is the 'protection of the environment'. The clause also requires that the top management shall assign the roles, responsibilities and authority for various levels in the organization and communicate to all concerned.

The following aspects should therefore be displayed by top management

- within the scope of the organizational context, the strategic plans of the organization and the OH&S policy and objectives are compatible and integrated.

- Provision of resources and that the OH&S can interact with the existing business processes

- Ensuring continual improvement can be achieved

- Supporting other relevant management roles to demonstrate their leadership as it applies to their areas of responsibility;

- Communicating objectives, aspects, and performance metrics and results to all stakeholders

In OHSAS 18001 the responsibility was delegated to a "management appointee" or "management representative" appointed by the management. Even though there is no requirement in the standard for Top management to appoint a Management Appointee, but still a competent person in the organization may be given responsibility for the establishment and implementation of the OH&S Management System but the Accountability for effective implementation lies with the top management, which requires a regular involvement and commitment by top management.

What the Organization Should Do:

"Top management shall demonstrate leadership and commitment with respect to OH&S management system" in Clause 5.1 clearly represents strengthened emphasis and expectations from top management to take accountability for the effectiveness of the OH&S and to ensure achievement of intended results. Top management therefore needs to have a clear view on what is their intended result of the OH&S.

To demonstrate leadership and commitment, there are specific responsibilities related to the management system in which top management should be personally involved or which top management should direct.

Important point to note is:

- Connection of OH&S to strategic direction thus leading to Integration of requirements into the organization's business processes.

- A knowledge of improvement in OH&S Performance on goals set by the organization for mitigating the significant impacts identified

What the Auditor Should Look For:

Auditors should audit the top management to verify that they take an active and leading role and understand their role in relation to the OH&S and are actively participating in promoting and supporting effective OH&S management in the organization. Auditors need to assess the understanding of top management functions in this respect. Evidence of leadership involvement may be verified through:

- Review of the Organizations strategy through their Vision and Mission statements, business plan/OH&S policy/objectives, including resource deployment.

- Involvement in objective setting, performance evaluation and follow-up. Top management should be aware of their critical OH&S issues and OH&S Performance through Continual Improvement Efforts.

- Records of meetings, action lists, and various means of communications (e.g. e-mails, newsletters, meetings with key employees),

- Clearly defined responsibilities and authorities

- Broad and active involvement from top management in management reviews wrt OH&S.

Top Management should be able to:

- Demonstrate knowledge of the OH&S objectives and provide an overview of where these objectives link with the organization's overall strategies.

- Demonstrate that leadership has been shown to the team in terms of communicating the importance of the OH&S, ongoing results, and progress versus stated OH&S objectives.

- Be familiar with the process of ensuring and encouraging continual improvement and demonstrate that this culture exists within the organization as a result of that leadership.

5.2 OH&S Policy

1. A well-formulated OH&S policy forms a basis for the objectives in the field of Occupational Health and Safety.

2. The policy spells out the measures to be taken and also highlight the relationship of these measures with the other organisation objectives such as quality or Safety policy. The policy should be short and precise, be published by the top management and made known to all employees.

An OH&S policy is a written document which expresses the organization's commitment to OH&S. The policy should influence all the activities including the selection of people, equipment and materials, the way work is done and how you design and provide goods and services.

The responsibility of establishing an OH&S policy lies with the Top management, and the policy should provide a framework for setting objectives. The standard now requires apart from a commitment to provide safe and healthy working conditions for the prevention of work-related injury and ill health, commitment to OH&S protection, and all factors contextual to the organization itself. The OH&S policy also requires commitment to eliminate hazards and reduce OH&S risks. Of course, the OH&S policy must provide a commitment to the continual improvement of the OH&S. Another important requirement added is commitment to consultation and participation of workers, and, where they exist, workers' representatives. Critically, the OH&S policy must be maintained as documented information, be communicated within the organization, and be available to all interested parties.

The purpose of establishing documented policies is for top management to communicate to the workforce its intention and direction.

Set a clear policy statement for safety and health. The policy statement can be brief, but it would mention:

- Commitment to continual improvement of the OH&S management system to enhance OH&S performance.

- Commitment to provide safe and healthy working conditions for the prevention of work-related injury and ill health and is appropriate to the purpose, size and context of the organization and to the specific nature of its OH&S risks and OH&S opportunities.

- Commitment to eliminate hazards and reduce OH&S risks,

- Commitment to consultation and participation of workers, and, where they exist, workers' representatives.

- Commitment to comply with applicable legal & other requirements.

- Commitment to Continually improve the OH&S Management System.

Organizations and Auditors should note the following:

The policy also needs to include

- Commitment to "protection of **Injury and Ill health**".

- Commitment to provide safe and healthy working conditions.

- Commitment to eliminate hazards and reduce OH&S risks.

- Commitment to consultation and participation of workers, and, where they exist, workers' representatives.

5.3 Organizational Roles, Responsibilities and Authorities

Top management has to ensure that roles, responsibilities, and authorities are delegated and communicated effectively. The responsibility shall also be assigned to ensure that the OH&S Management System meets the requirements of the ISO 45001:2018 standard and responsibility for communicating OH&S performance to top management.

As stated above, the term "Management Appointee" is no longer required. However, the areas of responsibilities are still to be assigned by top management for various levels of the organization and communicated.

Roles, Responsibility, Authority and Accountability

In order to effectively assign roles, responsibilities, and authorities it is useful to have a clear understanding of the concept's responsibility, authority and accountability.

Responsibility is basically an area in which a person is expected to act on his or her own accord. It is the obligation that subordinates have to their superiors to perform the duties of their jobs, *i.e.,* to achieve the desired outcomes for which they are accountable to their superiors. One way to determine a person's responsibility is to analyze what he or she can cause to occur. Let us say Raman is identified as the responsible person for implementing the OH&S management program on Eliminating a Significant Hazard identified. As such, it is Raman's *responsibility* to ensure that the actions listed in the OH&S management program are conducted in accordance with the established schedule to achieve the stated objectives and target. He does not have to undertake the actions himself; he can delegate the responsibility for each task to someone else. However, to carry out his responsibility, he must follow up with the individuals to whom he delegated the tasks and ensure that they are performing the tasks properly and in the appropriate time frame in accordance with their **Roles.**

Authority is the power to take actions and make decisions. Management authority is a form of influence and implies a right to take action, to direct and coordinate the actions of others. The delegation of authority permits decisions to be made more rapidly by those who are in more direct contact with an issue. Jobs can be divided into actions and decisions. Responsibilities and authorities should therefore be defined in terms of actions assigned to an individual and decisions that individual is permitted to make. In an organization, an individual should not be given the responsibility for performing a task, without also being given the authority to make decisions and act in a manner necessary to complete that task. Some tasks will probably be delegated with little authority for decision making (**e.g.,** the task must be accomplished according to a specified plan), while others will be delegated with much greater authority and decision power. Because Raman has the responsibility to eliminate the identified significant hazard, he should also have the authority to decide what level of effort, time, equipment, and other resources should be expended to reassess the effectiveness of the action taken and to decide how such an assessment will be conducted. Similarly, if Raman delegates a task to a subordinate, he should decide how much authority the task requires and ensure that he delegates the appropriate authority along with the responsibility for the task.

Accountability is control over the authority that has been delegated to immediate subordinates. This means that if a person delegates authority for a certain task, he or she is still accountable to see that the task **is**

accomplished, although the responsibility for the task has been transferred. For example, Raman delegated the task of managing the elimination of significant hazard to one of his subordinates. In this case, the responsibility for the task has been transferred, but Raman still retains ***accountability*** for the task and the overall OH&S management program.

What should the organization do?

Ensure that the roles and responsibility are clearly defined and communicated to all concerned. Identify the critical activities that are likely to affect the OH&S and define the responsibilities and authorities to enhance the OH&S performance.

What the Auditors should look for:

From an auditor's point of view, it is important to ascertain that personnel given responsibility have the authority necessary to effect changes, where required. Auditors should particularly look for critical activities that may have significant impact on OH&S and ask the concerned employees how their roles and responsibilities are ensuring control over those impacts. All personnel should be aware of their roles and responsibilities. Ask such employees about their authority in the implementation of those responsibilities.

5.4 Consultation and Participation of Workers

It is logical that those working closest to an OH&S risk will be more knowledgeable about the hazards and risks. Therefore, the participation of workers in the establishment, implementation and maintenance of an OH&S management system can play an important role in ensuring that the risks are managed effectively. ISO 45001 emphasizes the need for worker participation in the functioning of an OH&S management system, as well as requires that an organization ensures that its workers are competent to do their assigned tasks safely.

It is up to the organization to determine the best way(s) of ensuring effective consultation and participation and whether it needs to set up formal mechanisms such as health and safety committees. Once mechanisms have been determined, it is important that they are given full top management support. Consultation is about seeking workers' views, and considering them, before making a decision; participation is about joint decision-making, e.g. jointly assessing risks and agreeing actions, or deciding the organization's OHS policy and objectives. One way of consulting workers could be to ask them the Risk of activity, facility, equipments, tools being used by them and what do they feel is the opportunity for improvement. This will be a regular process since changes do happen in the operations over time.

The organization shall:

- provide mechanisms, time, training and resources necessary for consultation and participation;
- provide timely access to clear, understandable and relevant information about the OH&S management system;
- determine and remove obstacles or barriers to participation and minimize those that cannot be removed

Worker Consultation

Consultation is about seeking workers' views, and considering them, before making a decision, so consult workers for:

1. Determining the needs and expectations of interested parties;
2. Establishing the OH&S policy;
3. Assigning organizational roles, responsibilities and authorities as applicable;
4. Determining how to fulfill legal requirements and other requirements;

5. Establishing OH&S objectives and planning to achieve them;
6. Determining applicable controls for outsourcing, procurement and contractors;
7. Determining what needs to be monitored, measured and evaluated.

Worker Participation

Involve workers to

1. Determining the mechanisms for their consultation and participation;
2. Identifying hazards and assessing risks and opportunities;
3. Determining actions to eliminate hazards and reduce OH&S risks;
4. Determining competence requirements, training needs, and evaluating training;
5. Determining what needs to be communicated and how this will be done;
6. Determining control measures and their effective implementation and use;
7. Investigating incidents and nonconformities and determining corrective actions.

Note: Participation of managers also, who are impacted by work activities or other factors in the organization.

A small organization can include all workers in discussions and decision-making. For larger organizations, it can be more effective to consult with one or more workers' representatives than attempt to consult with large numbers of workers directly. Other mechanisms for consultation and participation include, for example, focused team meetings, workshops, worker surveys and suggestion schemes.

In some companies, when they have to purchase a new machine, a team of representative from Production, Maintenance and a worker would visit the supplier and review the machine to identify the hazards and give their suggestions on making it safe for operation and once the machine is received again it is handed over to the workers only after ensuring that there is no possibility of harm to health and safety of the personnel who will be operating the machine.

The organization should take into account the specific issue(s) being considered when choosing the best way to find out workers' views and how much time and resource should be devoted to consultation and participation on a particular topic. Relevant non-managerial workers affected by the issue should be involved in deciding what the best mechanism is to ensure their concerns are addressed and to encourage engagement.

The organization should ensure that processes for consultation and participation of workers include contractors and other relevant people, e.g. volunteers or people working in parts of the organization not covered by the management system but carrying out work under the organization's control. This can include, for example, consultation with contractors on issues such as dealing with hazards which might be new or unfamiliar to them.

6.0 Planning

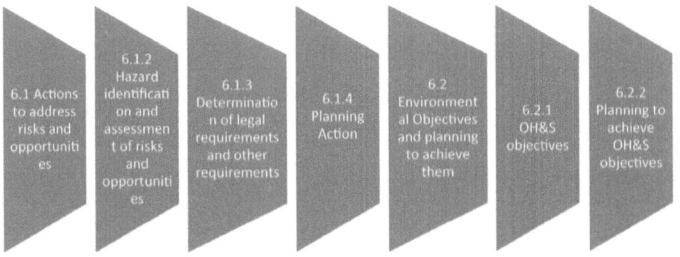

6.1 Actions to Address Risks and Opportunities

This clause states that the organization should identify the risks and opportunities associated with the organization and its workers, and the actions necessary to deal with these risks and opportunities. To achieve the Intended Outcomes, the process starts with applying an understanding of the context in which the organization operates, including issues that can affect the achievement of intended outcomes of the OH&S management system as per Cl. 4.1 and relevant needs and expectations of interested parties as per Cl. 4.2.

Also consider the legal and regulatory requirements, and the organization's OH&S hazards themselves. This outcome needs to ensure that the OH&S can achieve its intended outcomes and objectives, that any internal or external factors that may affect performance are controlled, and efforts made to achieve continual improvement in our OH&S performance.

In terms of emergency situations, the organization is required to determine any situations that may occur and have a resulting OH&S risk under the existing controls.

In brief, under Clause 6.1.1 identify risks and opportunities, i.e. issues that have or can have a significant hazard, whether adverse or beneficial. "The overall intent of Clause 6.1.1 is to ensure that the organization is able to achieve the intended outcomes of its OH&S systems, to prevent or reduce undesired impact on OH&S, and to achieve continual improvement.

There are three sources of risks and opportunities that need to be addressed in order to achieve its intended outcomes and achieve continual improvement:

a. OH&S hazards;

b. Strategic directions of the organization;

c. Contextual issues identified in Cl. 4.1 and Cl. 4.2 that may hinder the achievement of intended outcomes.

Workplace hazards can come from a wide range of sources. General examples include any substance, material, process, practice, etc. that has the ability to cause harm or adverse health effect to a person. See Table 1.

Table 1: Examples of Hazards and Their Effects

Workplace Hazard	Example of Hazard	Example of Harm Caused
Thing	Sharp object	Cut
Substance	Asbestos	Cancer
Source of Energy	Electricity	Electrocution
Condition	Wet floor	Slip and falls
Process	Fumes from Welding	Health effect
Practice	Coal mining	Silicosis
Behaviour	Bullying	Anxiety, Fear, Depression

Workplace hazards also include practices or conditions that release uncontrolled energy like:

- an object that could fall from a height (potential or gravitational energy),
- a run-away chemical reaction (chemical energy),
- the release of compressed gas or steam (pressure; high temperature),
- entanglement of hair or clothing in rotating equipment (kinetic energy), or
- contact with electrodes of a battery or capacitor (electrical energy).

What is Risk?

The standard defines "risk" as "the effect of uncertainty on objectives." From this definition, it is easy to envisage how any type of risk can have a negative effect on key performance indicators, which cause a negative effect on an organization's OH&S as a whole.

Risk can come in many forms, for example failure of a project, competition, technology problems, the effect on the OH&S from operations carried out by organization's activities, whether steam generation, emissions, or moving part of a machine. Therefore, it is sensible that the organization should give emphasis and importance to the hazards, which impact the OH&S.

Identifying "risk" within an Organization

Organizations use "risk assessment" to control and improve OH&S performance and prevent any hazards or risks affecting the organization's OH&S performance.

Risk – the combination of the likelihood of the occurrence of a harm and the severity of that harm.

Severity – the impact if the hazard occurs

Likelihood – the chance of something happening.

Note: In risk assessment terminology, the word "likelihood" is used to refer to the chance of something happening, whether defined, measured, or determined objectively or subjectively, qualitatively or quantitatively, and described using general terms or mathematically (e.g., a probability or a frequency over a given time period).

For example: the risk of developing cancer from smoking cigarettes could be expressed as:

- "cigarette smokers are 12 times (for example) more likely to die of lung cancer than non-smokers", or

- "the number per 100,000 smokers who will develop lung cancer" (actual number depends on factors such as their age and how many years they have been smoking). These risks are expressed as a probability or likelihood of developing a disease or getting injured, whereas hazard refers to the agent responsible (i.e. smoking).

Factors that influence the degree or likelihood of risk are:

- the nature of the exposure: how much a person is exposed to a hazardous thing or condition (e.g., several times a day or once a year),

- how the person is exposed (e.g., breathing in a fume, skin contact), and

- the severity of the effect. (e.g, one substance may cause skin cancer, while another may cause skin irritation. Cancer is a much more serious effect than irritation.

What is a risk assessment?

Risk assessment is the process where you:

- Identify hazards and risk factors that have the potential to cause harm (hazard identification).
- Analyze and evaluate the risk associated with that hazard (risk analysis, and risk evaluation).
- Determine appropriate ways to eliminate the hazard, or control the risk when the hazard cannot be eliminated (risk control).

What is an adverse health effect?

A general definition of adverse health effect is "any change in body function or the structures of cells that can lead to disease or health problems".

Adverse health effects include:

- bodily injury,
- disease,
- change in the way the body functions, grows, or develops,

- decrease in life span,
- change in mental condition resulting from stress, exposure to solvents, etc

Will exposure to hazards in the workplace always cause injury, illness or other adverse health effects?

Not necessarily. To answer this question, you need to know:

- what hazards are present,
- how a person is exposed (route of exposure, as well as how often and how much exposure may occur),
- what kind of effect could result from the specific exposure of a person
- the risk (or likelihood) that exposure to a hazardous material or condition would cause an injury, or illness or some incidence causing damage, and
- how severe would the damage, injury or adverse health effect be from the exposure.

The effects can be acute, meaning that the injury or harm can occur or be felt as soon as a person comes in contact with the hazardous agent (e.g., a splash of acid in a person's eye).

Some responses may be chronic (delayed). For example, exposure to a hazardous material may cause red swelling on the skin two to six hours after contact. On the other hand, longer delays are possible: cancer in the lining of the lung cavity, can develop 15–20 years after exposure to asbestos.

Once the hazard is removed or eliminated, the effects may be reversible or irreversible (permanent). For example, a hazard may cause an injury that can heal completely (reversible) or result in an untreatable disease (irreversible).

The way an organization identifies health and safety risks, using assessments of threats, impact, likelihood, etc., risk against an organization's OH&S performance needs to be evaluated by personnel who have knowledge of the processes and know about the prior abnormal issues that might have happened. Participation of workers in risk assessment is very helpful, since they have faced the issues during their working with the process over the period. But to make the system of identifying the risk more effective, involvement of all levels, particularly top management will give better results, rather than leaving it to one individual within the organization.

It should become normal for the senior management team to play an active role in identifying where the areas of risk lie. This should provide a more accurate and complete details of risk within your organization and your OH&S system.

The 45001:2018 standard seeks to **replace the "preventive action" with "risk based approach."** Therefore, the focus will move from preventive actions, (which may be less effective because they may be carried out by only certain individuals within an organization,) to risk based approach, which should be a more thorough process due to input and commitment from multiple stakeholders, with a heightened sense of importance due to the change in the standard.

The organization can also have risks and opportunities related to other issues (Clause 4.1), including OH&S conditions or needs and expectations of interested parties (Clause 4.2), which can affect the organization's ability to achieve the intended outcomes of its OH&S performance.

Some examples of risks and opportunities related to external/internal issues as per Cl. 4.1 or needs and expectations of interested parties as per Cl. 4.2, which are not necessarily derived from Cl. 6.1.2 Hazard identification and assessment of risks and opportunities and Cl. 6.1.3 Compliance Obligations.

Another requirement stated in Cl. 6.1.1 is that an organisation needs to identify potential emergency situations that may result in adverse OH&S hazards and other effects on the organisation.

Although risks and opportunities need to be determined and addressed, there is no requirement for formal risk management or a documented risk management process. It is up to the organization to select the method it will use to determine its risks and opportunities. The method may involve a simple qualitative process or a full quantitative assessment depending on the context. It is up to the organization to select the method by which its risks and opportunities are determined.

Documented information shall be maintained of the risks and opportunities that need to be addressed. There shall also be documented evidence to ensure that the process have been carried out as planned.

What are OH&S risks and OH&S opportunities?

While the OH&S impacts that result from your OH&S hazards could be an area of risk or opportunity for your business, they are not what is referred to in the ISO 45001:2018 standard when it discusses risks & opportunities. The reason that risks and opportunities are included in the planning section of ISO 45001:2018 is as follows:

- Ensure that the OH&S system can meet the intended outcomes
- Prevent or reduce undesired effects or potential effects from the organization
- Continual improvement

So, you need to identify the risks and opportunities that are present for your OH&S, decide what need to be addressed, and keep documentation of the risks and opportunities that you will address.

To understand the difference between External and Internal issues and their Risk and opportunity and the OH&S hazard analysis of your activities, products and services as per Cl. 6.1.2, take the example below.

Example 1 – When the ore of high quality, being extracted from the mine gets depleted, you would need to use a low quality, OH&S harmful ore in its place in the future. You could also find an opportunity to replace the current Technology with one that is more OH&S safe to use.

Example 2 – An organization decides to use painted metal parts in their assembly process to avoid rusting, they can go for ROHS compliant paints to reduce the impact of harmful chemicals being inhaled in the Paint process.

While these risks and opportunities are related to your OH&S hazards, they were not identifiable by OH&S hazard analysis of your activities, products and services.

So, there is a relationship between OH&S hazards and risks and opportunities in the OH&S system, but this is not the only place to find risks and opportunities. OH&S hazards are not the only risks and opportunities that you will be able to identify for your OH&S. Risks and opportunities can also arise from your Compliance Obligations (especially when they are changed/amended), information from your customers or market research, benchmarking your processes against other companies for improvement, suggestions from employees, or feedback from neighbours or other external interested parties.

How you identify risks and opportunities is up to you, but it is an important activity within your OH&S system. Risks and opportunities can bring in great ideas that can be used for the continual improvement of your OH&S Management System.

There is no requirement for you to have a documented system for identifying your risks and opportunities, nor do you need to formally track what they are or how you will address them. The only requirement for documentation with respect to risks and opportunities is to "maintain documented information about the risks and opportunities that need to be addressed." which means the organization shall establish a criteria for the selection of significant risks and maintain document to address the same.

After identifying the risks and opportunities that need to be addressed, you then also need to plan actions to address them as per Cl. 6.1.4. This can include using them in your decision of which OH&S objectives to put in place, but you are not required to have an OH&S objective for every risk or opportunity identified. When we identify significant hazard or Risk, they can be controlled by either making an Objective for Continual Improvement or by controlling the operation through an Operational Control Procedure.

It is not hard to see that identifying the risks and opportunities that are applicable to your business just makes sense when you have a management system and are trying to improve. It is only by managing your risks and taking action to gain the benefit of your opportunities that your business will be able to improve how it works.

The ISO 45001:2018 stresses the need for increased strategic risk management to replace and improve the current system that relies more on a "reactive" preventive action process.

The aim of "strategic risk management" is to focus the organization's top management and team to proactively assess and understand hazards that may cause risk to the OH&S system, and execute these actions before any OH&S hazard is felt, as opposed to a reactive control.

It is clear that the changes in the ISO 45001:2018 are designed to ensure that a proactive and strategic outlook is taken toward OH&S concerns. The key benefits to the OH&S system should come from identification and prevention of incidents, rather than reacting to events.

The swing toward strategic planning of how you assess OH&S hazards, by involvement of your management team, will create a fundamental change in OH&S performance. Consider that now it will become normal for your whole management team to think about any hazards that may affect your business and plan how these risks will be managed, or mitigated. Many OH&S "hazards," which in time become "incidents," are costly not only to the OH&S system, but also to your business.

OH&S hazards can create risks and opportunities associated with adverse OH&S risks, beneficial OH&S risks, and other effects on the organization. The risks and opportunities related to OH&S hazards can be determined as part of the significance evaluation or determined separately.

Compliance obligations can create risks and opportunities, such as failing to comply (which can damage the organization's reputation or result in legal action) or performing beyond its compliance obligations (which can enhance the organization's reputation).

The standard wants us to identify Other Risks and Other Opportunities as well.

Other Risks

Determine and assess the other risks (risks which are not directly related to the health and safety of people but which affect the OH&S management system itself and can have an impact on its intended outcomes).

Risks to the OH&S management system include:

- failure to address the needs and expectations of relevant interested parties;
- inadequate planning or allocation of resources;
- an ineffective audit programme;
- poor succession planning for key roles; and
- poor engagement by top management.

Other Opportunities

Opportunities to improve the OH&S management system can include:

- making top management's support for the OH&S management system more visible, e.g. through communications such as social media or highlighting OH&S performance in strategic business plans;
- improving the organizational culture related to safety and training;
- enhancing incident investigation processes;
- increasing worker participation in OH&S decisionmaking; and
- multi skill training

What the Auditors should Look For:

- Is the criteria for Risk & opportunity identification defined?
- What is the involvement of top management in the identification of Contextual issues and Needs and Expectations of Interested parties and are issues identified which can cause adverse effect on OH&S conditions,
- How the organization has chosen the needs and expectations of internal and external interested parties as Obligations to Comply

- Has the organization identified other risks and other opportunities also?

- Has the organization considered the bullying, work conditions, workload also in the assessment of risk and opportunities

6.1.2 Hazard identification and Assessment of Risks and Opportunities

6.1.2.1 Hazard Identification

ISO 45001:2018 requires organizations to consider OH&S hazards of its products, services, and activities that are within the organization's control. Changes or planned changes to services also need to be taken into account, as do any abnormal situations that may arise that are reasonable for the organization to predict – for example, if you are about to launch a new product then ensure that the controls are in place to ensure health and safety hazards are considered and controlled. The organization needs to maintain documented information on this clause and its elements, and communication to the concerned personnel, with effective frequency needs to be planned and undertaken. In terms of documented information, you have to ensure that the criteria used to define significant hazards is clearly established and understood by concerned personnel.

You have to identify OH&S hazards of all the activities under your control or you can influence, whether they are impacting positively or negatively. By knowing and understanding these you can control the negative impacts you have on the OH&S performance.

Identify the OH&S hazards that have significant risk. These OH&S hazards are the ways in which your company processes interact with the OH&S, but what does it mean to classify one of these interactions as significant? With no criteria listed in the ISO 45001 standard on what is significant, how do you decide what the definition should be? Here are a few things to consider when you come up with your definitions of which OH&S hazards are significant and which are not.

By identifying which of your OH&S interactions are the most important, and therefore worthy of further scrutiny and monitoring, you are able to prioritize what needs to have attention and what does not.

In this way you can assign the right resources to the right problems to get the best return on your OH&S investment. When only two hazards really matter, does it make sense to invest in managing all more than 100 OH&S interactions in a company?

Examples of Criteria for Significant hazards:

- **Legislative Requirement**: If you have a legal requirement to monitor, control, and manage an OH&S hazards, then this hazard is significant.

- **Potential for OH&S harm**: It depends on the activities that you perform. If you have a chemical process that uses cyanide, it has a greater chance of causing OH&S harm due to a spill than does a chemical process that uses alcohol. This is due to the nature of the chemicals involved and the effect that a spill could have on the OH&S around your facility.

- **Frequency**: How often you perform a process/activity and what is the frequency of a possible spillage or emission is also important. But there may be some operations that occur daily and may cause greater OH&S hazard, and therefore may require a better control. But you have to consider hazards of those activities also that do not occur frequently.

- **Stakeholders**: Company stakeholders are not just workers, management, and customers. The stakeholders also includes those living in your neighbourhood, so you need to consider what is important to them. You may have a process that emits hazardous fumes that may not be of particular concern to the plant because of control through exhaust fan, but if these fumes cause concerns to the neighbours, you may need to take steps to manage that OH&S hazard.

By determining the significant OH&S hazards of your processes/activities, you are trying to find the required controls. Focus on the identified significant hazards for control or possibly eliminate that hazard from your activities (by changing your process), which is beneficial to you and your OH&S system.

It is required to document the criteria used for determining the significant hazards.

The standard requires that while determining the OH&S hazards of its activities, products and services that it can control and those that it can influence, and their associated OH&S risks.

How the Organization should go about?

The best way to go about is to prepare a dynamic flow chart giving details of OH&S hazards of the activities, such as chemical, physical, biological or psychosocial.

Once the dynamic flow charts are prepared it will be easy to carry out the hazard identification analysis and on the basis of the existing control, identify the improvement projects. Do not just look at the hazards occurring under normal working conditions, but visualise the abnormal and potential emergency conditions and identify the controls for avoiding such abnormal or emergency situations and once such situation arises, mitigating plans. During hazard identification, the applicable legal requirements for various hazards will also be identified.

What the Auditors should look for:

- Weather the criteria for identifying significant hazards have been defined

- There is consistency in the organization in following the criteria

- Have the controls been established for the identified significant hazards. In establishing the controls, have they considered the hierarchy of controls.

- Is there consistency in the understanding and application of the criteria to identify the Significant hazards.

- Have they only considered the Normal activities for identifying the OH&S hazards or have envisaged potential Abnormal and Emergency situations as well.

6.1.2.2 Assessment of OH&S Risks and Other Risks to the OH&S Management System

The organization must establish, implement and maintain a process to:

- Assess OH&S risks from the identified hazards, whilst taking into account the effectiveness of existing controls;

- Determine and assess the other risks related to the establishment, implementation and maintenance of the OH&S management system.

An organization needs to apply the process of hazard identification and risk assessment to determine the controls that are necessary to reduce the risks of injury and/or ill health. The purpose of risk assessment is to address the hazards that might arise in the course of the organization's activities and ensure that the risks to people arising from these hazards are assessed, prioritized and controlled.

This is achieved by:

- Developing a methodology for hazard identification and risk assessment;

- Identifying hazards;

- Estimating the associated risk levels, taking into account the adequacy of existing controls, based on an assessment of the likelihood of the occurrence of a hazardous event or exposure and the severity of injury or ill health that can be caused by the event or exposure;

- Determining whether these risks are acceptable vis a vis the organization's legal obligations and its OH&S objectives;
- Determining the appropriate risk controls, where these are found to be necessary;
- Documenting the results of the risk assessment;
- Reviewing the hazard identification and risk assessment process on an ongoing basis.

There is no defined methodology for hazard identification and risk assessment. Each organization should choose the method that is appropriate to its scope, nature and size. The chosen approach should result in a comprehensive methodology for the ongoing evaluation of the organization's risks.

The risk assessment should involve consultation with, and participation by, workers and take into account legal and other requirements.

Risk assessment should be conducted by personnel with competence in risk assessment methodologies and techniques and appropriate knowledge of the organization's work activities. The organization should also consider risks which are not directly related to the health and safety of people, but which affect the OH&S management system itself and can have an impact on its intended outcomes. Risks to the OH&S management system include:

- Poor engagement by top management.
- Failure to address the needs and expectations of relevant interested parties;
- Inadequate consultation and participation of workers;
- Inadequate planning or allocation of resources;
- Poor succession planning for key roles;

6.1.2.3 Assessment of OH&S Opportunities and Other Opportunities for the OH&S Management System

Improvement In a companies' OH&S Management system can be carried out by identification of OH&S opportunities and other opportunities for the OH&S management system.

Some examples for OH&S Opportunities an organization can adopt to improve the OH&S Management system are

- Managing Director of a company was not fully involved in the OH&S management system, hence the HSE advisor of the company made an action plan to improve the involvement of the management in OH&S through shop floor audits and making the managing director the chairman of Safety committee.

- Evaluation of Compliance related to Safety was carried out manually in a company. The legal advisor of the company improved the system for compliance through implementation of Compliance software for better evaluation through notifications and compliance tracking tools.

- Only top management and core team were aware about the OH&S Management system implemented in the company initially. The Human resource identified opportunity for improvement by including to cover the entire organization.

6.1.3 Compliance Obligations

This is a relatively straightforward, but obviously vital part of the ISO 45001:2018 standard. The organization must decide what obligations are related to its OH&S aspects and how to best access them, decide how they apply to the organization, and take them into consideration when establishing, operating, and delivering continual improvement through the OH&S. Documented evidence needs to be recorded for these obligations, also.

There are two main requirements in this section:

1. Identify and have access to applicable compliance obligations:

This is the important first step of making sure that you know all of the legal requirements against the OH&S aspects that are applicable to your company. Remember that these can originate at a municipal, local, national, or even international level depending on the activities of your company. If you don't know that a specific legislation exists, you will very likely not meet the requirements of the legislation.

2. Determine how these obligations apply to your organization:

Equally as important as knowing that a law exists that could be applicable to your OH&S hazards is knowing if it actually applies to your situation. For instance, you may emit waste water into your local sewage treatment facility, which will have many laws associated with it; however, many of these could be related to chemicals that are not used in your process.

6.1.4 Planning actions

This Clause requires that the organization shall plan to take action to address its OH&S hazards, risks and opportunities, and compliance obligations. These also need to be implemented into the organization's OH&S system and associated business processes. The task of evaluating the effectiveness of these actions also must be considered, with technological, financial, and operational options.

6.2 OH&S Objectives and Planning to Achieve Them

6.2.1 OH&S Objectives

Having considered the identified OH&S hazards, risk and opportunities, and compliance obligations and identified Significant hazards, OH&S objectives should be established at appropriate levels and functions,. The characteristics of the set objectives are important, too. The objectives need to be consistent with the organization's strategic planning, OH&S policy, and should be measurable where possible, communicated effectively. It is mandatory that documented information is kept outlining this process and its outputs.

For deciding the objectives that the organization sets itself to achieve, following strategy will be helpful:

Providing Safe & Healthy Workplace with ISO 45001:2018

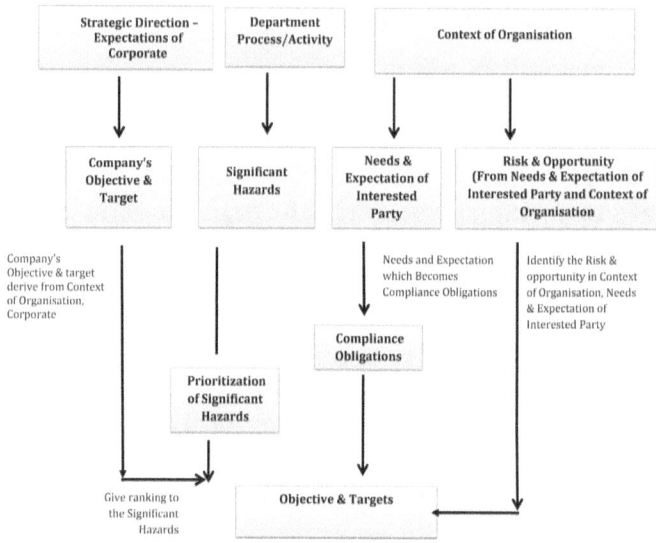

6.2.2 Planning to achieve OH&S objectives

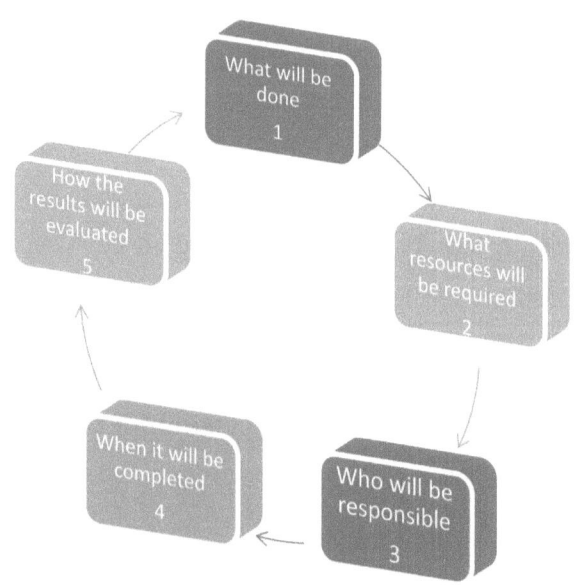

The standard requires planning of actions that need to be determined to ensure objectives can be achieved. This can be thought of in terms of what needs to be done, what is the target date, what resources are required to achieve it, and the responsibility for the achievement of objectives, how results will be measured and progress ensured, and consideration on how these objectives can be implemented into existing business systems.

What the Auditors should look for:

The auditors will ask for the controls over significant hazards identified and where the organization has made an objective for improvement in the OH&S performance, records of monitoring of the achievement of Objectives through Performance Indicators, such as, e.g.

- Objectives are measurable
- number of persons trained in OH&S hazards identification;
- quantities of specific hazardous fumes emitted, e.g. CO, VOCs, etc;
- Review of the records of actions taken, as planned
- Where Objectives are achieved, review for making more objectives

7.0 Support

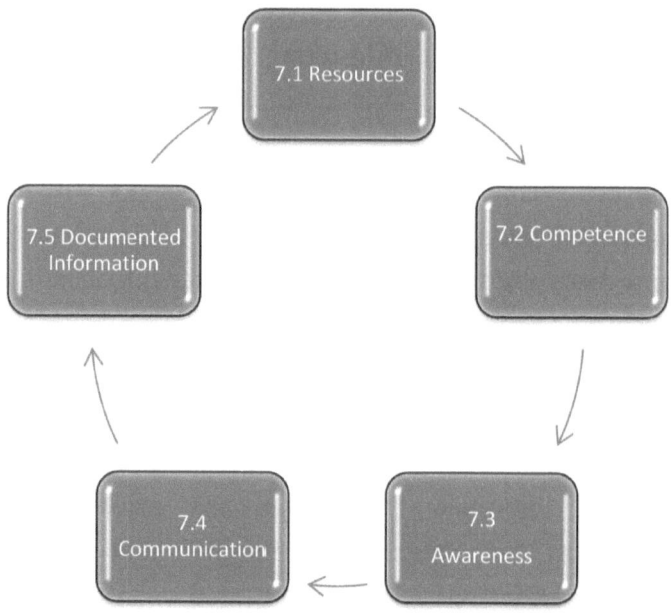

This clause begins with a requirement that organizations shall determine and provide the necessary resources to establish, implement, maintain and continually improve the OH&S system. Finally, there are the requirements for 'documented information'. 'Documented information' is a new term that replaces the references in the OHSAS 18001 standard to 'documents' and 'records. These requirements relate to the creation and updation of documented information and their control.

7.1 Resources

Having made plans to achieve the OH&S Objectives, the organization will identify the resource requirements for taking the planned actions. The organization shall ensure that resources to achieve stated objectives and show continual improvement are made available.

When determining the resources needed, the organization should consider:

- Financial resources
- Equipments
- Skill requirements

Resources and their allocation should be reviewed periodically, also during the management review to ensure their adequacy. Resources include human resources and specialized skills, organizational infrastructure, technology, and financial resources.

What the Organization should do?

The clause requires that resources be provided, the organization is therefore expected to conduct resource planning, and that forecasting be documented or that records of resource utilization be kept. Without such documentation, it will be difficult to demonstrate to an auditor that you have allocated adequate resources to implement the **OH&S** Management System.

What the Auditors should look for:

Does the company have the right people for implementing OH&S Management System? Does the company have specialized skills such as the competent personnel for an OH&S assessment?

Has the organization identified the resource requirements as per the Programmes to achieve the Objectives and for Monitoring & Measurement of Operational Controls?

Have they identified the requirements for Emergency Preparedness?

Do they have adequate money budgeted to make all of this possible?

7.2 Competence

Competence: Ability to apply knowledge and skills to achieve intended results

The standard requires that the organization shall:

a. determine the necessary competence of person(s) doing work under its control that affects its OH&S performance and its ability to fulfil its compliance obligations;

b. ensure that these persons are competent on the basis of appropriate education, training or experience;

c. determine training needs associated with its OH&S hazards and its OH&S management system;

d. where applicable, take actions to acquire the necessary competence, and evaluate the effectiveness of the actions taken.

All persons doing work under the control of the organization that affect or can affect its OH&S performance, including its ability to fulfil compliance obligations, should be competent based on training, education, experience, or a combination of these, as determined by the organization. As a minimum, the experience, training, and/or education of the individual must be as per requirement of the process, and that any training required is identified and provided to ensure that the required level of competence exists. Records of Competence need to be kept by the organization.

It is therefore required that the organization should ensure that the personnel have the **capability of applying the knowledge** gained through training and experience, as can be seen from the definition of Competence.

In essence, how does the organization ensure that employees (or contractual workers) who are involved in the processes, that have the potential for significant OH&S hazards, are able to act in such a way that those hazards are controlled? So, the process to ensure proper controls over activities having significant OH&S hazards will have to be controlled through competence, training, and awareness of the personnel involved.

For instance, if you have a chemical process that must maintain the concentration, then the concerned employee must know how this bath concentration shall be maintained.

If you require the operator to measure the concentrations and adjust the pH level through addition of an acid or base, then there is a level of chemical knowledge required to perform this action. It may not require the operator to have a particular education qualification, but he should have the knowledge to avoid the unwanted OH&S hazard of air emissions by properly maintaining the concentration, which could be through his training or experience.

Training: Once we have identified the competency required for an activity, to avoid potential significant OH&S hazards, we need to identify the gaps in required and available competencies. This is where training comes into place, especially when you are first implementing your OH&S management system and find that the people already doing a job do not have all of the competencies that are newly identified for the position.

Training can be given in different ways, sending employees in external programs offered by various training institutions, or on-the-job training where an experienced supervisor may impart training to an employee in correctly performing the job. The employee in the example above need not attain an educational qualification to perform the job, but he may need to gain an understanding of the processes required to safely perform the task.

7.3 Awareness

Even though desired competencies are available in the organization, there is a need to be make employees aware of

a. the OH&S policy;

b. the significant OH&S hazards and related actual or potential OH&S risks associated with their work;

c. their contribution to the effectiveness of the OH&S management system, including the benefits of enhanced OH&S performance;

d. the implications of not conforming with the OH&S management system requirements, including not fulfilling the organization's compliance obligations.

When employees understand the policy or procedures that they are to follow, they are much more likely to adhere to those requirements. Understanding that the consequences of not following the procedures may lead to OH&S issues and regulatory penalties that can lead to damaging the image of the company, they may be more likely to follow the rules.

Awareness of the proper procedure and the benefits of following it are important for compliance with the requirements. E.g. the person operating a chemical process may know that uncontrolled emissions from the process can be harmful to the human beings, if not properly controlled, but he may not understand what those controls need to be. Understanding of the roles is also very important. If a person does not understand what his role is, he is unlikely to perform that role properly.

What the Organization should do:

ISO 45001 specifies that you should keep records to show that competencies have been achieved through education, training, or experience. So, you need to ask yourself; for activities that can have a significant OH&S hazards, do I have everything I need to show that the people performing these activities are competent and trained to properly perform the tasks in such a way that the risk is avoided?

The organization must be able to assess, provide, and maintain the correct training and communication for the employees which are critical to the performance and objectives of the OH&S system. The organization should assess its own need of the level of competency necessary to achieve the desired results, including the level of induction training required when a new employee joins?

Once you have identified the job responsibilities of individuals within your organization with respect to OH&S performance, identifying the training and knowledge required is generally quite straightforward. But, for all the employees of the organization, at least following actions may be worth considering for the organization:

- An overview of the OH&S, its objectives,

- Ask team leaders to incorporate OH&S performance and updates into the regular team meetings.

- Ensure that there is a culture within the organization to promote information regarding the OH&S. This can be all Departmental Heads, for example: Regular education and awareness on departmental activities and their OH&S hazards and actions required for improving performance.

What the Auditors should look for:

Potential areas for Competence	Level being Audited	What competency/ capability expected
OH&S operations	Persons whose work activities involve significant OH&S Hazards	Awareness of how their work affects OH&S performance Knowledge of operating criteria that needs to be met in order to minimize adverse OH&S risks
OH&S management systems	**Internal Auditors**	The ability to develop and manage audit programmes to determine the effectiveness of the organization's OH&S management system

7.4 Communication

7.4.1 General

A system for internal and external communication needs to be established and records of communications need to be maintained. The standard has explicitly defined:

- on what it will communicate
- when to communicate
- with whom to communicate
- how to communicate.

S. No	Description of Communication	Mode of Communication	Responsibility	Frequency	Communicated To				
					All/ Conc. HoD's	OH&S Coordinator	Contractors	Customers	Interested Party

7.4.2 Internal Communication

The requirement of Internal Communication basically is that in the organization the required information, such as controls required and status of achievement of objectives, should be communicated at various levels and with various frequencies as deemed suitable, and to ensure that the nature and frequency of communication allows continual improvement in the OH&S Management System.

7.4.3 External Communication

Keeping in mind the compliance obligations and Performance indicators for the objectives set by the organization, it should be ensured that communication relevant to the OH&S takes place as per the established process, with the goal of ensuring that the objectives are met.

A process needs to be established for both internal and external communications, and mentioning that a method shall be "established and implemented" should the organization decide to communicate details of its significant OH&S hazards externally.

Communication: Who should deliver it?

Since the standard now clearly requires information on what to communicate, whom to communicate, how to communicate and the frequency of communication, a communication matrix can be prepared by the organization giving details as per standard's requirements. Every department will decide the four details required by the standard. A person can be nominated (May be Management Appointee) who will be responsible for the management, delivery, and logging of communication with respect to the OH&S. An equally key part can be shown by delivering vital communications to the top management; e.g. top management should be made aware of various Performance Indicators for OH&S improvement and on what improvement has taken place

As per the standard, the top management has an increased role in the risk management and strategic planning processes, it makes sense that external communication regarding OH&S hazards to external interested parties is given by the top management.

What the Organization should do:

The organization should consider different communication methods that would help in understanding and acceptance of the organization's OH&S management efforts and promote dialogue with interested parties. Methods of communication include, for example, informal discussions, organization open days, involvement in community events, websites and e-mail, press releases, advertisements and periodic newsletters, etc. It is to be ensured that all internal and external interested parties are correctly informed about the organization's compliance of OH&S, and its efforts for continual improvement of OH&S performance and OH&S. The organization should make decisions regarding the frequency and content of these communications. This will ensure that the organization is seen to be taking its communication duties seriously.

The standard requires that Organizations should retain documented information of its communications, as appropriate, in order to:

- understand the nature of various interested party engagements over time;
- recall the interested party communication, inquiries, or concerns;
- improve the organization's effectiveness in communication and in addressing the concerns of specific interested parties as needed.

What the Auditor should look for:

- The organization has a system to communicate
  - its significant OH&S hazards among the various levels and functions of the organization, as appropriate

- its OH&S objectives
- its relevant OH&S requirement(s) to external providers, including contractors
- relevant OH&S performance information both internally and externally, as determined by its communication process(es) and as required by its compliance obligations
- the results of internal audits are reported to relevant management
- Management's review includes consideration of communication(s) from interested parties
- That the organization is implementing the communication system made for communicating Internally and/or externally to ensure OH&S performance and proper implementation of OH&S management system.

7.5 Documented Information

7.5.1 General

The organization should develop and maintain adequate documented information to ensure that its OH&S management system is operating effectively, and is well understood by persons working under the control of the organization and other interested parties, and that processes associated with the OH&S management system are carried out as planned.

Through documentation, an organization should be able to demonstrate fulfilment of its compliance obligations and the organization's control requirements and their implementation in the organization.

In the standard where it says "shall maintain the documented information", it is referring to the requirement of a document and where it says "shall retain documented information" it means a record is expected there.

Documented information can be controlled in any medium (paper, electronic, photos and posters) that is useful, legible, easily understood and accessible to those needing the information contained therein.

Mandatory Documents

The organization should maintain the following as documented information:

- the scope of the OH&S management system (Cl. 4.3);

- the OH&S policy (Cl. 5.2);

- its identified risks and opportunities that need to be addressed (Cl. 6.1.1);

- the processes needed in Cl. 6.1.1 to Cl. 6.1.4, to the extent necessary to have confidence that these processes are carried out as planned (Cl. 6.1.1);

- its OH&S hazards and associated OH&S risks, the criteria used to
- determine its significant OH&S hazards, and its significant OH&S risks (Cl. 6.1.2);
- its compliance obligations (Cl. 6.1.3);
- information on the OH&S objectives (Cl. 6.2.1);
- information related to the operational control processes needed to meet OH&S management system requirements, to the extent necessary to have confidence that the processes have been carried out as planned (Cl. 8.1);
- the processes needed to prepare for and respond to potential emergency situations identified in Cl. 6.1.1, to the extent necessary to have confidence that the processes are carried out as planned (Cl. 8.2).

Mandatory Records

The organization should retain documented information as evidence (records) of the following:

- competence, as appropriate (Cl. 7.2);
- its communications, as appropriate (Cl. 7.4.1);
- monitoring, measurement, analysis and evaluation results, as appropriate
- compliance evaluation result(s)

- implementation of the audit programme, and the audit results
- the results of management reviews
- the nature of identified nonconformity and any subsequent actions taken, and the results of any corrective action

Other examples of documented information include descriptions of programmes and responsibilities, procedures, process information, organizational charts, internal and external standards, and site emergency plans.

7.5.2 Creating and updating

OH&S documentation should be available where and when needed, reasonably protected against damage or loss of integrity and identity, and the processes of distribution, retention, access, retrieval, preservation and storage, control and disposition are adequately provided for. It should be noted that documented information from external sources should be similarly controlled and handled, and that viewing and editing access levels should be carefully considered and controlled.

7.5.3 Control of Documented Information

Documented information can be effectively controlled by:

- developing an appropriate format that includes unique titles, numbers, dates, revisions, revision history;

- assigning the review and approval of documented information maintained by the organization to individuals with sufficient technical capability and organizational authority e.g. Concerned Department Heads;

- maintaining an effective distribution control system.

Do we need a Manual?

A manual is more of an administrative document. Making a simple OH&S management system manual that captures some important and required information in one place can make that information easy to locate for anyone who needs it. Since it is not an operational document, it does not contain any company confidential information. So a manual can be shared with other stakeholders and interested parties as a way of showcasing your OH&S.

Creating an OH&S to the requirements of ISO 45001 is not intended to be an effort in creating documentation. However, having documents that are practical and convey useful information in a straightforward way can help with communicating and maintaining the OH&S across your organization. The manual should capture significant information that require documentation as per ISO 45001 that can quite easily be useful in an OH&S manual.

Below are four small, but critical items that can quite easily form a useful OH&S manual:

1. Scope of the OH&S: The OH&S scope defines the coverage of boundaries of the OH&S management system within your company. The intent is to define and clarify the boundaries of the organization to which the OH&S will apply. This is particularly important for companies that are part of a larger organization where the OH&S is only applicable to one location. Once the scope is identified, all activities within that scope need to be identified, as they form a part of the OH&S.

2. OH&S policy: The intention of the OH&S policy is to provide intention of the company to prevent pollution, meet compliance standards for any applicable legal requirements, and continually improve the OH&S. The policy provides a focus for the employees of the company to work in a direction, as it conveys the OH&S goal of the organization.

3. Roles, Responsibilities & Authorities: While much of the roles, responsibilities and

authorities for the OH&S processes may be captured in the documentation for each process, some of the overall responsibilities may be given in the manual.

4. OH&S Elements & their interactions: Each company has differing processes, procedures, and OH&S interactions. So, two companies may not have exactly the same elements in their OH&S management systems, and even if the elements are similar, they may interact differently. So, in the manual give details of what are the main elements of your specific OH&S, and how they interact?

In ISO 45001 there are very few pieces of information in the OH&S management system that need to be documented, and none of these are required documented procedures. There are a couple of documents like policies, plans, and records that need to be written, but no written procedures are explicitly mandated by the standard. So, how do you decide which of the procedures in the ISO 45001 standard should be documented in your OH&S management system?

The intent of this requirement is for the organization to assess which of their activities/processes have a significant hazard, and to have a documented method of controlling this activity/process. This way, all employees who are involved in that process/activity can have a common understanding of what is needed to ensure that a significant risk from the activity/process is avoided. It is important to note that this is only applicable for significant hazards; if you do not have a process with a significant risk, then it is not mandatory to have a procedure for all operational controls.

A very good rule of thumb is to document a procedure when there is a high chance that there will be mistakes when it is not documented. This is particularly applicable to procedures used for planning the response during an emergency. These procedures can be critical to ensuring that everyone knows how to respond, what training is required and maintained for the responders, and what other people should do when the emergency occurs, even if this is to just be out of the way of the emergency responders.

Another time to consider documenting a procedure is when you want to ensure that the review criteria and the assessed output are consistent across the organization. For example, you don't need to have a procedure on how you identify and classify your OH&S hazards, but if you want to make sure that all process owners look at the same items to assess what an hazard is (and more importantly, that all personnel assess what is significant in the same way), then writing down a procedure that identifies these specific requirements is important.

Some processes of an OH&S that are very commonly documented include:

- How you identify and classify your OH&S hazards
- How you identify and keep applicable legal requirements up to date
- How you determine competence, awareness, and training
- How the documents and records of the OH&S are controlled
- Emergency plans and how they will be executed should an identified emergency occur
- How nonconformity, corrective actions are carried out
- How an internal audit is conducted
- How a management review is performed

By documenting only the procedures that you will need for your OH&S to properly function and improve, you can avoid the trap of having a lot of wordy documents that are difficult to read and maintain. If your procedures contain the information that is needed, without a lot of extra information that is not used, you will also increase the chances that your documentation will remain relevant and be used by the employees who need to know what is written. In this way you can keep your OH&S implementation lean, useful, and relevant.

8.0 Operation

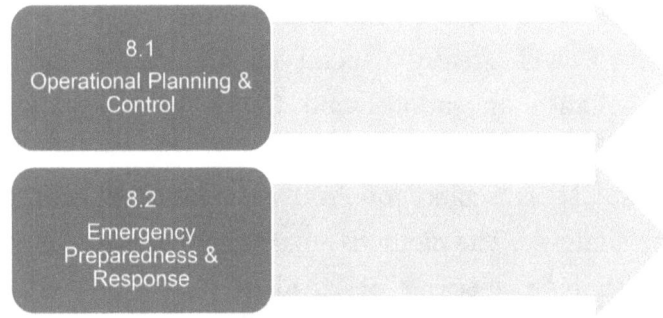

This clause provides guidance on the operational planning and control requirements relating to the OH&S management system.

This clause encompasses the following:

- Operational planning and control;
- Eliminating hazards and reducing OH&S risks;
- Management of change;
- Procurement;
- Emergency preparedness and response.

This clause deals with the implementation of the processes that enable the organization to meet their OH&S intended results, policies and objectives.

8.1 Operational Control and Planning

While the standard acknowledges that operational control will greatly depend on the size, nature, compliance obligations, and OH&S aspects of an organization, the scope is given to the individual organization to plan and ensure the intended results are achieved. The methods suggested by the standard are that processes be designed in such a way that consistency is guaranteed and error eliminated (Mistake Proofing), technology is used to ensure effective & efficient controls, and it is ensured that personnel are trained and are competent.

Processes should be performed in an agreed and defined manner; those processes should be measurable, and the documented information should match the requirements to ensure operational control.

Processes related to the external service providers (Outsourced Processes) must also be established and controlled. Appropriate measures must be made to define and control the competency of outsourced service providers, including consideration of their resources, knowledge, competence, and ability to meet objectives. Consideration must be made for the degree to which the organization and the outsourced provider share process control, and also how control can be made through established elements such as the existing procurement process. The standard also recognizes that the degree of control the organization has over an outsourced product or service can vary from absolute, if taking place onsite, to very little, if the activity takes place remotely. However, it is suggested that there are factors that nonetheless should be considered.

8.1.1 Operational Controls Planning

Once it has gained an understanding of its OH&S hazards, the organisation should implement the operational controls that are necessary to manage the associated risks and comply with applicable OH&S legal requirements.

Operational planning and control of the processes are established and implemented to enhance occupational health and safety, by eliminating hazards or, if not practicable, by reducing the OH&S risks to levels as low as reasonably practicable for all relevant operational areas and activities.

The organisation can plan, implement and control its operational processes by establishing operating criteria and control the processes in accordance with these operating criteria. The operational controls selected should be maintained and evaluated periodically for their continuing effectiveness.

Control Over Outsourced Processes

Category of Process	Name of Outsourced Agency (M/s)	Selection Criteria*	Evaluation Method*	Controls* (Documents to be obtained)	Appraisal & Frequency	Process Owner	Approving Authority

May be attached in separate sheet, if needed

Examples of operational control of processes include:

- Use of procedures, work instructions, process maps and systems of work;
- Monitoring key characteristics and stipulated operating criteria;
- Ensuring the competence of workers;
- Establishing preventive or predictive maintenance and inspection programmes;
- Developing specifications for the procurement of goods and services;
- Applying controls related to contractors and other visitors to the workplace;
- Ensuring compliance with legal and other requirements or manufacturers' instructions for equipment;
- Applying engineering and administrative controls;
- Adapting work to workers by defining or re-defining how the work is organised, processes and working environments or by adopting an ergonomic approach when designing new, or modifying workplaces, equipment, etc.

When planning and developing operational controls, priority should be given to controls with higher reliability in preventing work-related injury and ill health.

Examples of processes needed include, but are not limited to those for:

- Consultation and participation of workers;
- Hazard identification and risk and opportunity assessment;
- Determination of, and compliance with, legal and other requirements;
- Planning, implementing and maintaining OH&S objectives;
- Training;
- Communication;
- Control of documented information;
- Management of change;
- Procurement;
- Contractor management;
- Outsourcing;
- Emergency preparedness and response;
- Monitoring, measurement, analysis and performance evaluation;

- Internal audits;
- Management review;
- Incident investigation;
- Nonconformity and corrective action.

What processes do you need to comply with the operational control requirements, and how do they relate to OH&S hazards? Do you really need to have processes for every hazard identified? Is operational control really necessary? The answers to some of these questions might surprise you.

OH&S hazards are the ways in which your organization controls an activity/process, and these are critical in the assessment of which operational controls are needed for ISO 45001:2018. The requirements of section 8.1 hinge on three main criteria for creating an operational control procedure:

- Linkage of operations activities with significant OH&S hazards
- Lack of control could deviate from the OH&S policy
- Lack of control could deviate from the objectives and targets

So, when you have an operation that has significant OH&S hazards, you need to identify and plan that operation to be consistent with your OH&S policy, and your OH&S objectives and targets, to make sure they are carried out to specified conditions. This is done by establishing, implementing, and maintaining a documented process to control these situations and stipulate operating criteria in the procedure. This is clear when you have an operation where you have a significant OH&S hazards. The standard recognizes the need of a documented control procedure for the significant hazards identified for a process.

So, it is clear that you do not need a documented procedure for every activity you do to meet these requirements, only those with significant OH&S hazards. The question that remains is if it is possible to have a situation where none of these operations have significant OH&S hazards. It is true that the organization needs to identify what constitutes *significance* for their identified OH&S hazards; however, for certification purposes these criteria need to be justified to the auditors of a certification body who will review your OH&S management system for compliance with the requirements of ISO 45001.

So, when is operational control necessary in an ISO 45001 OH&S management system? If you have identified operations with an OH&S hazard that you deem to be significant, then you need to have procedures to control these operations.

Remember, the reason for implementing an OH&S management system is not to please a certification body or to find ways to avoid documentation. An OH&S management system is there to help your organization to identify and control your activity/process and reduce any negative impact, if any.

What the Organization should do:

The organisation must co-ordinate the relevant parts of its OH&S management system with those of any other organisations with which it shares its workplace.

The organisation needs to maintain and retain documented information to the extent necessary to have confidence that the processes will be carried out as planned.

- Prepare Operational Control Procedures for the hazards/risks and give training to concerned personnel for implementation.

- While preparing Operational Control procedures for the activities of the organization consider controls over the outsourced processes.

- Prepare a list of processes that have been outsourced and identify the controls for selection, evaluation and assessment of the outsourced suppliers of products and services.

What the Auditors should look for:

- Knowledge of Operational Controls to the concerned employees.
- Identifying the controls, starting from design of the product, procurement, processing.
- Look for identified outsourced processes and control of the Organization on those outsourced product/service suppliers.

Clause 8.1.2: Eliminating Hazards and Reducing OH&S Risks

The organisation should apply the hierarchy of control measures for the reduction of OH&S risks. The hierarchy of controls provides a structured approach to controlling OH&S risks. Each control is considered less effective than the one above it. It is customary to combine several controls in order to effectively reduce the OH&S risks to a level that is as low as reasonably practicable.

When deciding what is reasonably practicable, best practices and technological options should be considered, in addition to financial, operational and business requirements.

If new or improved controls are required, their selection should be in accordance with the hierarchy of controls whereby priority is given to the elimination of hazards, where practicable, followed by other alternatives, with the usage of PPE as the last resort.

Follow the following hierarchy of controls:

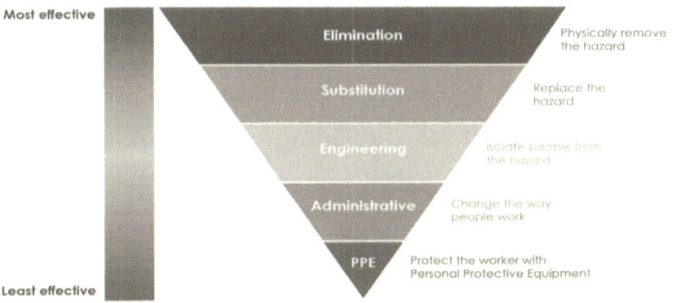

Elimination: removing the hazard; discontinuing the use of hazardous chemicals, applying ergonomic approaches when planning new workplaces such as the use of mechanised instead of manual packaging; eliminating monotonous work practices; removing fork-lift trucks from an area.

Eg; In a city, a number of over bridges were made and, on the bridges, pillars were installed for fixing lights. Whenever, light bulbs got fused, a truck full of red cones with a number of labourers to stop the traffic and then a cherry picker would pick an electrician to the top of the pillar to change the bulbs. This would mean a traffic jam for 2–3 hours, just to change a few fused bulbs. Then someone thought of "Eliminating the hazard of going on height to change the bulbs".

A system has been made by which a person presses a button at the bottom of the pillar so the bulb holder comes down. The person changes the bulb and pushes the button so the bulb holder goes on top of the pillar again. So they eliminated the hazard of going to height for replacement of bulb.

Substitution: replacing the hazardous with less hazardous such as replacing solvent-based paint by water-based paint, changing slippery floor tiles, or lowering voltage, pressure or temperature requirements for equipment.

E.g.: A textile company was using CS_2 (Carbon disulphide) for black dying of white cotton cloth. In the process H_2S gas was being generated but workers were not using any nose mask. The company planned to substitute CS_2 by another chemical so that H_2S emission can be avoided. They were able to find a substitute, a chemical from Maize which avoided the H_2S emissions and gave the desired result also for black dying of cotton cloth.

Engineering controls/work reorganisation: isolating people from hazard; implementing collective protective measures (e.g. isolation, machine guarding, ventilation systems); addressing mechanical handling; reducing noise; protecting against falls from height by using guard rails; reorganising work to avoid lone working, unhealthy work hours, workload; reducing the effect of monotonous work by rotating workers.

Administrative controls including training: conducting periodic safety equipment inspections; conducting training to prevent bullying and harassment; managing health and safety co-ordination with subcontractors' activities; conducting induction training; providing instruction on how to report incidents and nonconformities; changing the work patterns (e.g. shifts) of workers; managing a health or medical surveillance programme for workers who have been identified as at risk (related to hearing, hand-arm vibration, respiratory disorders, etc.); giving appropriate instructions to workers (e.g. entry control processes, emergency); safety signs. Sometimes if elimination, substitution or engineering control is not possible to control a hazard, at least we can warn the workers of the possibility of an incident so that they are careful. E.g. when a person is cleaning a floor, he puts a warning board "Wet Floor" so that persons moving in the area would know that there is a possibility of slip and fall.

Personal protective equipment (PPE): providing adequate PPE, including clothing and instructions for PPE utilisation and maintenance (e.g. safety shoes, safety glasses, hearing protection, gloves). Even though it is very important to use the necessary PPEs but when we have identified the possibility of a hazard, we must follow the above hierarchy. If as a first step we start thinking about the usage of PPEs, we are not able to think of eliminating the hazard or following the other possibilities.

In applying the hierarchy of controls consideration should be given to the relative costs, risk-reduction benefits and reliability of the available options.

Clause 8.1.3: Management of Change

The organisation is required to establish a process for the implementation and control of planned temporary and permanent changes that influence its OH&S performance such as:

- New products, processes or services;
- Changes to work locations, working conditions, processes, procedures, equipment, or the company's organisational structure;
- Changes to applicable legal and other requirements;
- Changes in knowledge or information concerning hazards and associated risks
- Developments in knowledge and technology

The company is required to control both temporary and permanent changes, to review the consequences of unintended changes and, where applicable, to take action to mitigate any adverse effects that might arise as a result of the occurrence of change.

The overall purpose of the management of change process is to minimise the introduction of new hazards and risks into the workplace as a result of changes in:

- Technology
- Plant and equipment
- Facilities
- Work practices and procedures
- Design specifications
- Raw materials
- Company personnel
- Standards or regulations

Depending on the nature of any anticipated change, the company must use a suitable methodology for assessing the risks and the opportunities that might arise as a result of the change.

The company must ensure that new, unforeseen hazards are not introduced, or the risk profile increased as a result of the introduction of the change. Where the company decides to implement the change, it must ensure that all affected employees are properly informed and are competent to cope with the change.

The management of change process should include consideration of the following questions to ensure that any new or changed risks are acceptable:

- Have new hazards been created?
- What are the risks associated with the new hazards?
- Have the risks from other hazards changed?
- Could the changes adversely affect existing risk controls?
- Have the most appropriate controls been chosen, bearing in mind usability, acceptability and both the immediate and long-term costs?

Clause 8.1.4: Procurement

Clause 8.1.4.1: General

The organisation must establish, implement and maintain a process to control the procurement of products and services in order to ensure their conformity to its OH&S management system.

Procurement processes should be used to control potential hazards and reduce OH&S risks associated with the purchase and introduction of products, hazardous chemicals, raw materials, equipment and ancillary services into the workplace. The process should also address the need for consultation and communication on the procurement process with interested parties such as workers, contractors and visitors. Prior to procuring goods and services, the organization should identify procurement controls that: – Identify and evaluate potential OH&S risks associated with products, materials, equipment and services – Require products, materials, equipment and services to conform to OH&S objectives – Define needs for information, participation and communications – Verify that any procured equipment, installations and materials are adequate before being released for use by workers – Ensure goods are delivered to specifications and are tested to ensure they work as intended – Communicate and make available usage requirements, precautions or other protective measures Organization must establish a process and determine controls for achieving reduction in OH&S risks.

The organisation should ensure that purchases are safe for use by workers by confirming that:

- Equipment is supplied in accordance with a technical specification such as CE-marking and, where appropriate, is tested to ensure that it functions as intended;

- Equipment is supplied in accordance with legal requirements;

- Where appropriate, risk assessments are carried out in advance of the use of the equipment;

- Installations are commissioned to ensure that they function as designed;

- Materials are supplied in accordance with technical specifications;

- Usage requirements, precautions or other protective measure are communicated and made available to workers, contractors and others who could be adversely affected.

Clause 8.1.4.2: Contractors

The organisation must co-ordinate its procurement process with its contractors, in order to identify hazards and to assess and control the OH&S risks arising from:

- Contractors' activities and operations that impact or have the potential to impact the organisation;

- The organisation's activities and operations that impact or have the potential to impact contractors' workers;

- Contractors' activities and operations that impact or have the potential to impact other interested parties in the workplace such as visitors or the public.

Contractor activities include the full gamut of services provided to organisations including maintenance, construction, facilities, security, cleaning, waste management and a number of other functions. Contracting activities can also encompass consultants, accountants, administrators and other specialist service providers.

The organisation must ensure that the requirements of its OH&S management system are met by contractors and their workers. The procurement process should define and apply occupational health and safety criteria in the selection of contractors, ideally in contract documents or service level agreements (SLAs).

How the organisation manages often diverse and complex relationships with contractors can vary, depending on the nature and extent of the service provided and the hazards and risks associated with it. When co-coordinating with contractors, the organisation should consider the reporting of hazards between itself and its contractors, controlling worker access to hazardous areas, and procedures to follow in emergencies.

The organisation should specify how the contractor will co-ordinate its activities with the organisation's own OH&S management system processes (e.g. those used for lock-out tag-out, confined space entry, exposure assessment and process safety management, etc.) and for the reporting of incidents.

The organisation must verify that contractors are capable of performing their tasks before being allowed to proceed with their work, by, for example:

- Reviewing the contractor's OH&S management system documentation such as risk assessments, procedures/work instructions/method statements, OH&S manual/Safety Statement;

- Confirming that the contractor's OH&S performance records are satisfactory (review notifiable accidents or dangerous occurrences, improvement or prohibition notices);

- Assessing the contractor's understanding of its OH&S legal and other obligations;

- Determining that qualification, experience and competence criteria for workers are specified and have been met (e.g. through training);

- Resources, equipment and work preparations are adequate and ready for the work to proceed;

- Checking the contractor's emergency and evacuation plans and procedures and level of preparedness in the event of an emergency;

- Reviewing the contractor's process for incident investigation, and reporting of nonconformities and corrective actions;

- Assessing contractor OH&S consultation, communication and participation with and of its workforce and other relevant interested parties including the organisation;

Clause 8.1.4.3: Outsourcing

Outsourcing (or sub-contracting) is the employment of an external organisation to perform one or more processes in the OH&S Management System. This can include system processes (e.g. internal auditing, etc.) as well as operational processes (e.g. welding, recruitment, component sterilisation, etc.).

Responsibility for conforming to the requirements of the ISO 45001 is vested in the organisation, because the outsourced process remains part of the organisation's OH&S Management System, including the necessary controls exerted on the outsourced process for OH&S purposes. The organisation must establish appropriate controls both to ensure that the external provider understands what is required of it and to give itself assurance that these are being pursued in a responsible way.

The organisation must verify that its outsourcing arrangements are compliant with legal requirements and are consistent with achieving the intended outcomes of the OH&S management system.

The type and degree of control to be applied to outsourced functions and processes must be defined within the OH&S management system and should be based on criteria such as:

- The ability of the external organisation to meet the organisation's OH&S management system requirements;

- The technical competence of the organisation to identify hazards, assess risks, determine appropriate controls and understand its obligations vis a vis OH&S legislation;

- The potential effect the outsourced processes may have on the organisation's ability to achieve the intended outcomes of its OH&S Management System;

- The extent to which the outsourced process or function is shared;

- The capability of the organisation to achieve the necessary controls through the application of its procurement process;

- Opportunities for improvement.

So you have to show your control over outsourced activity by asking the organization performing your activity about controls to ensure they are taking care of health & safety of their personnel and meeting applicable legal requirements.

Controls can include contractual requirements, training, inspections and risk assessments.

8.2 Emergency Preparedness and Control

Emergency preparedness and control is a key element of mitigation of OH&S risk. The standard informs us that it is the responsibility of the organization to be prepared, and a number of elements should be considered and planned for any OH&S potential emergencies.

Plan – We need to identify the potential emergency scenarios through Aspect Impact Assessment/Risk Assessment that can have a severe impact on the organization such as, but not limited to, Release of Harmful Gas into the atmosphere, Leakage of any hazardous/toxic chemicals into the land, water drain, Fire.

Do – Actions to mitigate those emergency incidents must be developed, as well as internal and external communication methods and appropriate methods for emergency response. Consideration of varying types of OH&S incidents needs to be considered, as does root cause analysis and corrective action procedures to respond to incidents after they occur. Regular training needs to be considered and undertaken, and assembly routes and evacuation procedures defined and communicated. Lists of key personnel and emergency agencies (think clean up agencies, local emergency services, local OH&S office or agency) should be established and made available, and it's often good practice to form partnerships with similar neighbouring organizations with whom you can share mutual services and provide help in the event of an OH&S incident.

Check – Periodic testing of the emergency procedures needs to be done by the organization to see effectiveness of the trainings & plans designed to respond to an emergency. These can be done in form of Fire drills, Mock Drills, Desktop reviews of the plans, complete evacuation drills etc. The organization should test emergency procedures for all types of emergencies identified.

Act – The organization should carry out root cause analysis and take corrective actions for the discrepancies/issues identified during the testing of the emergency procedures and the same should be communicated to all the personnel responsible.

All the document information of the Emergency plans, Mock Drills, Trainings etc. needs to be maintained and retained by the organization.

What the Organization should do:

- Have an Emergency plan.
- Identify the potential Emergency situations.
- Prepare a schedule of Mock drills to be conducted, considering different Emergency scenarios
- Maintain records of mock drills
- Review Emergency plan after actual emergency or mock drill

What the Auditor should look for:

- Understanding among employees on their response to Emergencies
- Review of Emergency plan after any emergency or mock drill
- Mock drill records to see whether they identify anomalies in the emergency response system during their mock drill

9.0 Performance Evaluation

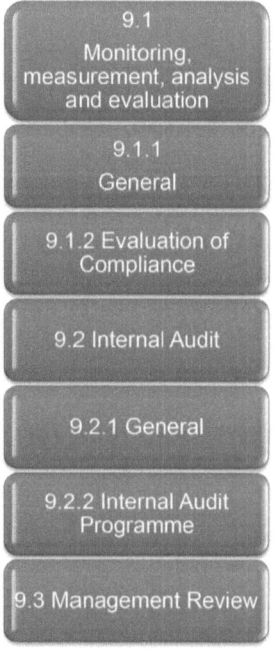

Performance monitoring and measurement are important in managing OH&S issues in the organization. They provide feedback on what is happening so that we can shape appropriate actions to respond to changing circumstances. They provide information on:

- what is happening around us,
- how well we are doing,
- what has happened so far,

- warning of impending problems or dangers that we may need to take action to avoid OH&S issues.

Arrangement for performance monitoring and measurement should:

a. be based on the organisation's identified OH&S risks, Significant hazards, the commitments in the OH&S policy and the OH&S objectives; and

b. support the organisation's evaluation process, including the management review.

As a general recommendation, determine what information you need to evaluate the OH&S performance and the effectiveness of your OH&S. Work backwards from this 'information need' to determine what to measure and monitor, when, who and how. Organizations should also revisit their audit programme in particular to ensure that it meets the new requirements.

Performance monitoring and measurement should:

a. be used as a means of determining the extent to which OH&S policy and objectives

b. are being implemented and risks are controlled;

c. include monitoring, under normal conditions and abnormal/emergency situations; and be recorded.

Monitoring should contain the elements necessary to have a proactive system and should include:

a. monitoring of the achievement of specific plans, established performance criteria and objectives;

b. the systematic inspection of work systems, premises, plant and equipment;

c. surveillance of the working environment, and

d. compliance with applicable national laws and regulations, collective agreements and other commitments on OH&S to which the organisation subscribes

The OH&S performance evaluation is an internal process and mechanism that should enable continual management of reliable and verifiable information in order to determine whether the OH&S management system meets criteria defined by the management of the organization. The Performance evaluation uses indicators for gathering the information, and compares current and previous performance with criteria for OH&S performance established by the organization itself.

As in any other situation that requires a systematic approach, you can't go wrong if you apply the Plan-Do-Check-Act cycle (see also Plan-Do-Check-Act in the ISO 45001 standard. The steps should be taken according to the following figure:

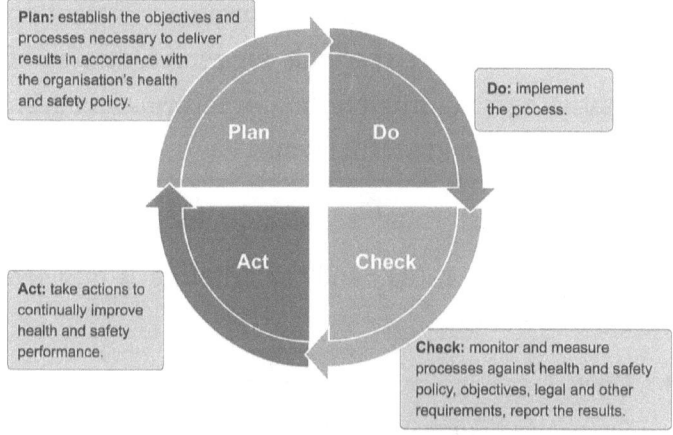

Figure: Application of PDCA cycle in OH&S Performance Evaluation

Planning the OH&S Performance Evaluation

If you want your OH&S performance evaluation to really work, you must incorporate it into the everyday activities of your organization. The OH&S Performance Evaluation must be based on your significant OH&S hazards, your own criteria for evaluation of OH&S performance, and requirements of the interested parties.

When planning the OH&S performance evaluation, you need to take into account the overall spectrum of your activities, products, and services, as well as other things that create the context of your organization.

The scope of the Performance Evaluation will facilitate the selection of the Performance Evaluation indicators, which are the tools for representation of qualitative and quantitative data, or information in an understandable and useful form.

Examples of performance indicators include:

- the emission of CO_2, and the criterion is targeted emission of CO_2.
- Dust level in an area measured in terms of Suspended Particulate Matter (SPM)
- Training on OH&S measured as man hours of training per person per month
- Noise in an area measured as dB

Reviewing and improving the PERFORMANCE EVALUATION

The OH&S performance of the organization and its results must be reviewed periodically in order to identify possibilities for improvement. This review can contribute to actions of the management toward improvement of OH&S condition.

Phases in reviewing it and its results can include reviewing of:

- Achieved effectiveness of OH&S protection
- Appropriateness of selected OH&S performance indicators
- Appropriateness of criteria of OH&S protection
- Sources of data, and methods for collection of data

The management commitment is essential for conducting the Performance Evaluation. The OH&S performance evaluation should be appropriate to the size, location, and type of organization, as well as to its needs and priorities. The information created through the Performance Evaluation can help the organization to:

- Identify trends in its OH&S performance indicators
- Increase effectiveness and efficiency
- Identify strategic opportunities.

The OH&S performance evaluation can give you real insight on whether your OH&S system is effective or not, and what needs to be improved.

9.1 Monitoring, Measuring, Analysis and Evaluation

9.1.1 General

The organization not only has to monitor & measure the OH&S performance, but should consider its significant hazards, compliance obligations, and operational controls.

Once you have established your OH&S management system according to ISO 45001:2018, you need to determine if it is working. To achieve that, organization needs to evaluate its OH&S performance against its OH&S Policy, OH&S Objectives and Targets, and other criteria that you have established for the OH&S performance.

If the organization wants the OH&S performance evaluation to work, they must incorporate it into the everyday activities of their organization. The OH&S performance evaluation must be based on the significant OH&S hazards, their own criteria for evaluation of OH&S performance, and requirements of the interested parties.

The measurement results needs to be compared against defined criteria; for example, the OH&S performance indicator can be emission of VOC, and the criterion is targeted emission of VOC. This comparison can indicate the progress in performance of OH&S protection. These results can be useful for understanding why the criteria for OH&S performance are or aren't met.

Organization shall establish, implement and maintain a process for monitoring, measurement and evaluation. Shall determine what needs to be monitored and measured, including...

- Criteria against which the organization will evaluate OH&S performance
- Methods for monitoring, measurement, analysis, and evaluation, as applicable, to ensure valid results
- When the monitoring and measuring shall be performed
- When the results from monitoring and measurement shall be analyzed, evaluated and communicated

Examples of what needs to be monitored and measured can include:

1. Progress on meeting policy commitments, achieving objectives & continual improvement
2. Occupational health surveillance of workers & work environment
3. Work related incidents, injuries, ill health

4. Effectiveness of operational controls
5. OH&S performance

What the Organization should do:

The organization should ensure that Monitoring and measuring is conducted under controlled conditions with appropriate processes for assuring the validity of results, such as:

- Selecting sampling and data collection techniques;
- Calibration of measuring equipment;
- Use of competent personnel;

The results of monitoring and measurement should be analysed and used to identify nonconformity, adherence to compliance obligations, performance trends and opportunities for continual improvement.

What the Auditors should look for:

- Understanding in the organization about the performance indicators
- Understanding about the operational criteria for various activities
- Knowledge of the trends of OH&S performance for the objectives set by the department

- Calibration of measuring equipments
- Analysis of root cause for non-conformances observed during analysis of operations

9.1.2 Evaluation of Compliance

The evaluation requirements will vary from organization to organization based on factors such as size, compliance obligations, type of activity, needs and expectations of interested parties etc. but a periodic evaluation is always required. If the result of a compliance evaluation reveals that a legal requirement is not being met, the organization needs to assess what action is appropriate. Where a non-compliance is identified by the OH&S and corrected, it does not automatically become a non-conformity.

What the Organization should do:

- Identified relevant interested parties and their relevant needs and expectations for OH&S
- Identified the chosen obligation from the needs and expectations of interested parties and evaluation of compliance of those obligations
- Identified the applicable Legal and other requirements and evaluation of compliance

What the Auditor should look for:

- Awareness of chosen compliance obligations among staff and evaluation records
- Knowledge of applicable Legal and other requirements for significant hazards, particularly when it is a concern for the organization
- Records of evaluation of compliance obligations

9.2 Internal Audit

9.2.1 General

Internal audits should be given same importance as Pre-Dispatch Inspection i.e. identifying all NG products in house and not let any rejections/failures at Customer end. Organizations should carry out very in-depth Internal audits to identify their own vulnerabilities and improve upon them so that there are not any nonconformities during customer/external audits.

Internal audits and auditors should be independent and have no conflict of interest over the audit subject, the standard reminds us, and it should be noted that non-conformities should be subject to corrective action.

When considering the results of previous audits, the results of previous internal and external audits and any previous non-conformities and resulting actions to correct them should be taken into account.

9.2.2 Internal audit program

The 45001:2018 standard refers us to ISO 19011:2018 for the internal audit program, but when you are establishing your program there are several rules you can subscribe to in order to ensure your program is effective. Decide what is reasonable for you, whether that is bi-annual, quarterly, or whatever you deem suitable.

Like management reviews, most of the organizations carry out internal audits once or twice a year, which might be complying with standard requirements, however, the frequency of the internal audits should be based on the following,

1. OH&S Management System Maturity,
2. Customer Complaints,
3. Compliance Obligations
4. Issues related to interested parties
5. Number of Significant OH&S Hazards,
6. OH&S Incidents,
7. Results of Previous Internal Audits.

Keep in mind that this schedule can be changed, preferably through management review and leadership guidance in the event of changes that necessitate additional internal audit.

The audit includes an evaluation of the organisation's OH&S elements or a sub-element of these, as appropriate.

The audit should cover:

- OH&S policy;
- role, responsibility and accountability;
- competence and training;
- OH&S documentation;
- communication;
- system planning, development and implementation;
- prevention and control measures;
- management of change;
- emergency preparedness and response;
- performance monitoring and measurement;
- audit;
- management review;
- non conformity and corrective actions;
- continual improvement; and
- any other audit criteria or elements that may be appropriate.

Audits should be conducted by competent persons, internal or external to the organisation that is independent of the activity being audited. The internal auditor should be selected and trained by the organisation in a manner to ensure objectivity and impartiality of the audit process.

Effectiveness of Internal Audits

Given also that continual improvement is a theme that underpins the 45001:2018 standard, it seems reasonable to assume an internal audit should be used to drive continual improvement, but is this always the case?

Many organizations view internal audit processes in different ways, whether it is simply a "box ticking" exercise or an unpleasant event where an auditor trying to identify maximum Non-Conformities. It should not be considered a mandatory Evil; however, it should be viewed as a real "opportunity for improvement" of your OH&S management system, its performance and the effect your organization has on the environment itself.

Approach for an effective Internal Audit

In compliance with the 45001:2018 standard, your Management Team will have identified OH&S risks, set targets based on compliance obligations, and set key performance indicators to meet and eventually be improved upon – all designed to ensure that we meet the intended results of our organization's OH&S management system. The internal audit is now your chance to ensure that not only are these targets met, but that they are relevant, and meet all the needs of current legislation and internal needs. Before embarking on an internal audit on your OH&S management system, it is advisable to carefully examine the targets and standards you are trying to meet.

It is very important that the internal auditors competence is mapped and are trained to carry out internal audits. Other than training, it is also important for organizations to have a criteria for selecting the internal auditors as the wrong selection of internal auditors can dissolve the entire system of internal audit.

Steps for Internal Audit

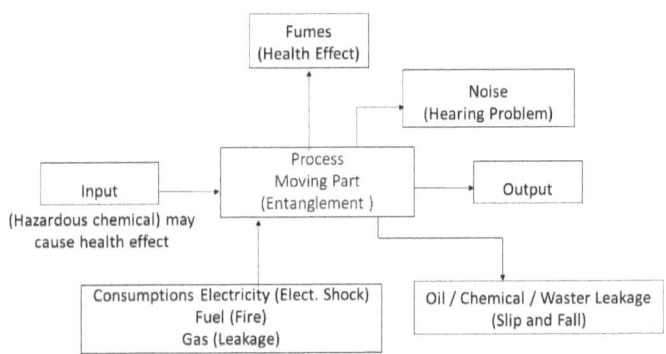

1. It is necessary for Internal Auditor to first understand the process and its OH&S hazards. For this ask the auditee to make a flow chart of the process and detail the OH&S hazards from the process as below.

2. Review the Risk & Opportunities and Hazards Identification done by the department and check whether all the hazards shown in the flow chart have been considered under Normal, Abnormal and Emergency situations.

3. Have they identified the controls

4. Has the criteria for determining significance clearly defined and understood by those who have carried out the Hazards Identification

5. How the Workers have been consulted/ participated in Hazard Identification and Risk Assessment (HIRA)

6. Is there consistency in the approach of HIRA by different departments

7. Have they carried out risk assessment of their contextual issues and identified controls, where significant OH&S risk identified

8. Have they identified their OH&S Performance indicators and are monitoring the same

9. Have the concerned personnel been trained on their operations, OH&S hazards of their activities, controls required, dealing with abnormal and emergency situations

What the Certification Body Auditors should look for:

- Competence of Internal Auditors
- Their independence
- Reports submitted by Internal auditors
- Has root cause analysis for non-conformities done?
- How the reports have been closed
- Is there a repetition of non-conformities?
- Are the details of audit reports discussed in the Management Review meeting?
- Are they periodically reviewing the Internal and External issues and Needs and expectations of workers and other interested parties?
- How they are ensuring the consultation and participation of workers in deciding OH&S policy, OH&S objectives, controls over outsourced processes, contractor selection, incident investigations as per Cl. 5.4

9.3 Management Review

It should be noted that, contrary to popular belief, the management review need not be done all at once; it can be a series of high-level or board meetings with topics tackled individually.

The standard requires top management to review the suitability, adequacy and effectiveness of the OHSMS at planned intervals. It is an opportunity for senior management to critically evaluate the performance of the OH&S management system to ascertain if it continues to be:

- Suitable: Is the management system in line with its operation, its culture and its business systems;

- Adequate: is the management system being implemented appropriately;

- Effective: Is the management system achieving its intended outcomes.

The Management review inputs are identified by the standard keeping in mind the totality of the OH&S management system.

The Cl. 9.3 requirements set out what is required from an organization in terms of management review, and what input criteria need to be established to demonstrate the organization's commitment in meeting the intended results. As one can expect, an organization's top management should play a key role in this, but the increased emphasis on leadership in the standard means that top management will be expected to understand, demonstrate and be able to talk about how the OH&S is measured and improved, and how effective this has been.

Management review may be one of the activity through which the commitment of the top management can be demonstrated and formally recorded in a manner that leaves all stakeholders assured of the team's commitment to OH&S improvement.

The findings from management review should be consistent with the organisation's commitment to continual improvement and should include any decisions and actions related to possible changes to:

a. OH&S performance;

b. OH&S policy and objectives;

c. Risk assessment and risk control processes;

d. Current levels of risk and the effectiveness of existing control measures;

e. Adequacy of resources (financial, employee, material);

f. an assessment of the foreseeable changes in the needs and expectations of interested parties

What the Auditors should look for:

All the agenda point as per the standard Clause 9.3 considered during Management Review meeting

Is the organization deciding about follow up actions by various departments for continual improvement?

10.0 Improvement

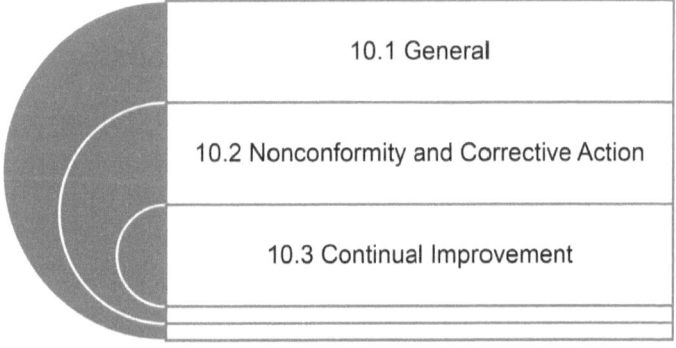

The organisation must actively seek out and, where possible, realise opportunities for improvement that will facilitate the achievement of the intended outcomes of the OH&S management system.

The organisation should consider the results from analysis and evaluation of its OH&S performance, evaluation of compliance, internal audits and management review, when taking actions to improve its performance.

Improvement can arise from corrective action, continual improvement, breakthrough change, innovation and re-organisation.

Due to the new structure and risk focus of the standard, there are no specific requirements for preventive actions in this clause. However, there are some new more detailed corrective action requirements. The first is to react to nonconformities and incidents, and take action, as applicable, to control and correct the nonconformity and deal with the consequences. The second is to determine whether similar nonconformities exist, or could potentially occur elsewhere in the organization, leading to appropriate corrective actions across the whole organization if necessary. Although the concept of preventive action has evolved there is still a need to consider potential nonconformities, albeit as a consequence of an actual nonconformity. The requirement for continual improvement has been extended to ensure that the suitability and adequacy of the OH&S as well as its effectiveness are considered in the light of enhanced OH&S performance.

Many companies go overboard with documentation in the belief that they need to document every single process that is in place in their organization, without realizing that this is not necessary to meet the requirements of the ISO 45001 standard. In the standard there are several mandatory processes, but there are no requirements of documented procedures. The standard also identifies many records that need to be retained, which are generated by the processes of the OH&S management system.

What are the key improvements? ISO 45001:2018 now requires:

- OH&S management to be more prominent within the organization's strategic direction
- A greater commitment from leadership
- The implementation of proactive initiatives to protect the environment from harm and degradation, such as sustainable resource use and climate change mitigation
- The addition of a stakeholder-focused communication strategy It also allows for easier integration into other management systems thanks to the same structure, terms and definition

Preventive Measures Versus Strategic Risk Management

The ISO 45001:2018 standard relies on risk assessment along with actions to minimize the impact that a business has on the OH&S performance; however, how the above are expected to be performed are not specified. The 45001:2018 standard seeks to replace the "preventive action" with "Risk based approach". Therefore, the focus will move from preventive actions, which may be less effective because they may be carried out by only certain individuals within an organization, to "Risk based approach", which should be a more thorough process due to understanding of the needs and expectations of multiple stakeholders, with a heightened sense of importance due to the change in the standard. Also, if you have to provide a corrective action, you are reacting to an event that has already occurred. The new standard aims to prevent these incidents described by the use of risk based approach.

The aim of "strategic risk management" is to focus the organization's top management and team to both spend more time assessing, researching, and understanding hazards that may present risk to the environment, and execute these actions before any OH&S impact is felt, as opposed to during or after.

10.1 General

Outputs from management reviews, internal audits, and compliance and performance evaluation should all be used to form the basis for improvement actions.

Improvement examples could include corrective action, reorganization, innovation, and continual improvement programs.

The organization needs to identify Improvement actions to achieve desired results for the OH&S through action plans established from Management Review

Outputs, Internal Audits, Performance & Compliance evaluations to ensure continual improvement in the system.

The organization should consider Technological advancements, Innovative solutions, Management & Engineering controls etc. as Improvement actionable points to achieve the desired result.

Outputs from management reviews, internal audits, and compliance and performance evaluation should all be used to form the basis for improvement actions. Improvement examples could include corrective action, reorganization, innovation, and continual improvement programs.

10.2 Nonconformity and Corrective Action

The organisation should have a process in place for reporting and investigating incidents and other nonconformities, and for taking action to correct them and deal with their consequences. Separate processes may exist for incident investigations and nonconformities reviews, or these may be combined as a single process. It is imperative that root cause analysis be carried out on the incident or nonconformity in order to take appropriate action to prevent a recurrence.

Prevention of incidents is a key facet of the OH&S, and this is specifically addressed in the definition of organizational context and assessing risks and opportunities.

Due to the introduction of the High Level Structure and Risk Based Thinking in the revised standard, there are no specific requirements for preventive actions in this clause.

However, there are some new more detailed corrective action requirements. First action to take is Correction/Immediate actions/React to non-conformities, as applicable, to control the nonconformity and deal with the consequences.

The second is to determine whether similar nonconformities had existed in the past, or could potentially occur elsewhere in the organization, leading to appropriate corrective actions across the whole organization if necessary. Although the concept of preventive action has evolved, however, we still need to identify the potential nonconformities, as a consequence of an actual nonconformity. The scope of the Continual Improvement has been extended to ensure the effectiveness and efficiency of OH&S Management System in the light to enhance the OH&S Performance.

Once nonconformity is identified, it should be investigated to determine the cause(s), so that corrective action can be focused on the appropriate part of the system. An organization should consider what actions need to be taken to address the problem, and/or what changes need to be made to correct the situation.

- Incidents: near misses, injuries and ill-health and damage to property or equipment that could lead to OH&S risks; such as a broken leg, asbestosis, hearing loss;

- Nonconformities: protective equipment not functioning properly; failure to fulfil legal requirements; prescribed processes or procedures not being followed; contractor behaving in an unsafe manner on-site.

When an incident or nonconformity occurs, the organisation must react in a timely manner, act to control and correct it and deal with the consequences.

It must evaluate the need for corrective action to eliminate the root cause of the incident or nonconformity in order to ensure that it does not recur or occur elsewhere in the organisation by:

- Investigating the incident or reviewing the nonconformity;

- Finding out what caused the incident or nonconformity;

- Finding out if similar incidents have occurred, if nonconformities exist, or if they could potentially occur.

The evaluation of the need for corrective action should be carried out with the active participation of workers and the involvement of other relevant interested parties.

The aim of an incident investigation is to determine what happened, why it happened, and what can be done to prevent it from happening again. This means not only considering the immediate causes, but also the underlying or root causes and taking corrective action to address these causes.

Almost all incidents have multiple causes. These can be related to a range of factors, including human behaviour and competency, the nature of the tasks and processes, equipment or management of the organisation. The investigation should identify all areas that need improvement including improvements to the OH&S management system and propose appropriate corrective actions.

The level of investigation should be proportionate to the potential health and safety consequences of the incident. The incident should be recorded and reported internally and, where appropriate, reported externally to regulatory bodies. Where practicable, the investigation should be led by a person independent of the activities being assessed and should include a worker or workers' representative.

Examples of corrective actions

- Eliminating hazards;
- Substituting with less hazardous materials;
- Redesigning or modifying equipment or tools;
- Implementing Poka-yoke/Mistake proofing
- Developing and implementing procedures or improving processes;
- Improving the competence of affected workers;
- Changing the frequency of use of equipment, etc.;
- Using personal protective equipment.

Corrective actions should be appropriate to the effects or potential effects of the incidents or nonconformities encountered.

Root cause analysis refers to the practice of exploring all of the possible factors associated with an incident or nonconformity by ascertaining what happened, how it happened and why it happened, to provide an input for what can be done to prevent it happening again.

When determining the root cause of an incident or nonconformity, the organisation should use methods appropriate to the nature of the incident or nonconformity being analysed. The focus of root cause analysis is prevention. Root cause analysis can identify multiple contributory failures, including factors related to communication, competence, fatigue, equipment or documentation.

While root cause analysis is being performed, the organisation may also have to undertake immediate but temporary actions to prevent the occurrence of the same nonconformity or incident. This would form part of the corrective action.

What the Organization should do:

The organisation should

- Review existing OH&S risk assessments for continued suitability (e.g. did the risk assessment anticipate the occurrence of the incident or nonconformity);

- Decide on and implement any action needed, including corrective action, in accordance with the hierarchy of controls (reference clause 8.1.2) and the management of change (reference clause 8.1.3);

- Assess OH&S risks that relate to new or changed hazards, prior to taking action;

- Review the effectiveness of any action taken, including corrective action (e.g. the extent to which the implemented corrective actions adequately control the root cause);

- Make changes to the OH&S management system, if necessary such as updating a process map or procedure.

- On observation of a non-conformity every department should record it, correct it, carry out root cause analysis and take corrective action to avoid recurrence

- Inform management through coordinator so that it is communicated to all departments

- Analyse the trend of non-conformances and take action for continual improvement

The organisation should retain documented information as evidence of:

- The nature of the incidents that occurred or nonconformities encountered, and any subsequent actions taken;

- The results of any actions and corrective actions taken, including their effectiveness.

The organisation should communicate this documented information to relevant workers, and where they exist, workers' representatives, and other relevant parties.

It is worth noting that the investigation and reporting of incidents without undue delay can enable hazards to be eliminated and associated OH&S risks to be minimised as soon as possible.

What the auditors should look for:

- Knowledge of the trends of non conformity in the departments
- Root cause analysis and corrective action taken on non conformities
- Review of the Non conformities and effectiveness of corrective action in Management Review meeting

10.3 Continual Improvement

Why continual improvement?

The concept of continual improvement is embodied in all management systems based on annex SL such as ISO 9001, ISO 14001, ISO 27001, ISO 22301 and of course ISO 45001.

Actions which an organisation might take with a view to achieving continual improvement in the suitability, adequacy and effectiveness of its OH&S management system include:

- Enhancing OH&S performance;

- Promoting a culture that provides support to the OH&S Management System;

- Promoting the participation of workers in the identification and implementation of actions for continual improvement of the OHS Management System;

- Communicating the relevant results of continual improvement to workers, and where they exist, workers' representatives;

- Maintaining and retaining documented information as evidence of continual improvement

First, it is important to understand again what is meant by continual improvement and why we want to work toward this in the OH&S. The term *continual improvement* is used to identify the need to systematically improve different processes within the OH&S in order to provide improvements overall. It is unreasonable to expect that every process within the OH&S will be improving all the time, so continual improvement is used to plan, monitor, and realize improvement in some processes that have been identified for improvement.

While there are many ways that continual improvement can be planned within an OH&S, two of the main processes identified in the requirements of ISO 45001 are the use of OH&S objectives and risk-based thinking. Through the proper use of these two processes you can see great benefits from continual improvement in your OH&S.

Examples of continual improvement opportunities may include:

- New technology;
- Good practices that arise internally in the organisation and externally to the organisation;
- Suggestions and recommendations from interested parties;
- New knowledge and understanding of occupational health and safety-related issues;
- New or improved materials;
- Changes in worker capabilities or competence;
- Achieving improved performance with fewer resources.

How do OH&S objectives work toward continual improvement?

OH&S objectives are intended to be planned for improvements to your OH&S processes, a main contributor to continual improvement. Here is an example of how this might work within an OH&S:

1. An organization creates an objective to reduce (Respirable particulate matter) PM 10 and (Particulate matter size that can be carcinogenic) PM 2.5 levels on their shop floor.

2. A target of 25 reduction within 6 months is set for this objective.

3. A program with the following activities is started to achieve this goal:

    - Study and identify processes generating dust of size PM 10 and PM 2.5.

    - Install dust collectors or filters to reduce the dust levels.

    - Monitor the dust levels and if the targets are not being achieved, study further and take actions accordingly.

Through applying the resources to accomplish this OH&S objective, OH&S improvement is achieved.

How does risk-based thinking work toward continual improvement?

Like the use of OH&S objectives, the application of risk-based thinking can also improve the processes of the OH&S. In OHSAS 18001 the preventive action process is used when you identify a problem that could occur in a process before it happens. When you identify a problem that could occur, and correct the process before the problem can happen, you are once again improving the OH&S. In ISO 45001:2018 preventive action has been removed, but the concept of risk-based thinking has been incorporated to identify risks before they happen. Here is an example of how risk-based thinking could work:

1. You are planning to give contract to an organization for gas cutting work in your plant.

2. With the help of workers, supervisors and Maintenance personnel, identify the risk involved keeping in mind that errors could be made with this process due to the manual nature of the treatment, which is dependent on an operator and the machinery being used by the contractor working at your premises.

3. Address this risk and take action to ensure safe working by the contractor personnel, that may include, a Work Permit to be taken from

your authorised person before starting the gas cutting work, and of course, the work permit will include all controls for the risks identified. This eliminates the potential error.

Some continual improvement is also seen with the corrective action process; however, the problem has already solved with a corrective action. This is still improvement, but it occurs after an OH&S incident has occurred and is less preferable to identifying the risk and addressing the problem before it happens

Conclusion

The standard ISO 45001:2018 provides organizations with guidance to mitigate OH&S risk and reduce impacts of their activities leading to OH&S protection. Every requirement of the standard is truly effective and their understanding and proper implementation can benefit your organization, in many ways. Certification/Registration of ISO 45001:2018 will bring benefits in many ways, such as enhancing company image, motivating the employees, and also financial benefits to your organization through improved efficiency and high morale. All of these benefits are closely related to your organization's ability to deliver satisfaction to your customer, and fulfil the expectations and wishes of your stakeholders, while protecting the Health & Safety of your personnel.

Bearing all this in mind, can your organization afford not to have ISO 45001:2018? So, what are you waiting for? Be a leader, do not look at others but initiate the process for Certification/Registration immediately and get the benefits.

Bibliography

1. ISO 45001:2018, *OH&S management systems — Requirements with guidance for use*

2. BS 45002-0-2018 Occupational health and safety management system Part 0: General guidelines for the application of ISO 45001

3. ISO 19011:2018, *Guidelines for auditing management systems*

4. CSA Z1002 Standard "Occupational health and safety – Hazard identification and elimination and risk assessment and control

Correspondence Between ISO 45001:2018 and OHSAS 18001:2007

ISO 45001:2018		OHSAS 18001:2007	
Clause title	**Clause number**	**Clause number**	**Clause title**
Introduction			Introduction
Scope	1	1	Scope
Normative references	2	2	Normative references
Terms and definitions	3	3	Terms and definitions
Context of the organization (title only)	4		
		4	OH&S management system requirements (title only)
Understanding the organization and its context	4.1		
Understanding the needs and expectations of workers and other interested parties	4.2		
Determining the scope of the OH&S management system	4.3	4.1	General requirements

ISO 45001:2018		OHSAS 18001:2007	
Clause title	**Clause number**	**Clause number**	**Clause title**
OH&S management system	4.4	4.1	General requirements
Leadership (title only)	5		
Leadership and commitment	5.1		
OH&S policy	5.2	4.2	OH&S policy
Organizational roles, responsibilities and authorities	5.3	4.4.1	Resources, roles, responsibility and authority
Consultation and participation of workers	5.4		
Planning (title only)	6	4.3	Planning (title only)
Actions to address risks and opportunities (title only)	6.1		
General	6.1.1		
Hazard identification and assessment of risks and opportunities	6.1.2	4.3.1	Hazard identification and assessment of risks
Compliance obligations	6.1.3	4.3.2	Legal and other requirements
Planning action	6.1.4		

Correspondence Between ISO 45001:2018 and OHSAS 18001:2007

ISO 45001:2018		OHSAS 18001:2007	
Clause title	**Clause number**	**Clause number**	**Clause title**
OH&S objectives and planning to achieve them (title only)	6.2	4.3.3	Objectives, targets and programme(s)
OH&S objectives	6.2.1		
Planning actions to achieve OH&S objectives	6.2.2		
Support (title only)	7	4.4	Implementation and operation (title only)
Resources	7.1	4.4.1	Resources, roles, responsibility and authority
Competence	7.2	4.4.2	Competence, training and awareness
Awareness	7.3		
Communication (title only)	7.4	4.4.3	Communication
General	7.4.1		
Internal communication	7.4.2		
External communication	7.4.3		
Documented information (title only)	7.5	4.4.4	Documentation
General	7.5.1		
Creating and updating	7.5.2	4.4.5	Control of documents
		4.5.4	Control of records
Control of documented information	7.5.3	4.4.5	Control of documents
		4.5.4	Control of records

Correspondence Between ISO 45001:2018 and OHSAS 18001:2007

ISO 45001:2018		OHSAS 18001:2007	
Clause title	**Clause number**	**Clause number**	**Clause title**
Operation (title only)	8	4.4	Implementation and operation (title only)
Operational planning and control	8.1	4.4.6	Operational control
General	8.1.1		
Eliminating hazards and reducing OH&S risks	8.1.2		
Management of change	8.1.3		
Procurement	8.1.4		
Emergency preparedness and response	8.2	4.4.7	Emergency preparedness and response
Performance evaluation (title only)	9	4.5	Checking (title only)
Monitoring, measurement, analysis and evaluation (title only)	9.1	4.5.1	Monitoring and measurement
General	9.1.1		
Evaluation of compliance	9.1.2	4.5.2	Evaluation of compliance
Internal audit (title only)	9.2	4.5.5	Internal audit
General	9.2.1		
Internal audit programme	9.2.2		

ISO 45001:2018		OHSAS 18001:2007	
Clause title	**Clause number**	**Clause number**	**Clause title**
Management review	9.3	4.6	Management review
Improvement (title only)	10		
General	10.1		
Incident, Nonconformity and corrective action	10.2	4.5.3	Nonconformity, corrective action and preventive action
Continual improvement	10.3		
Guidance on the use of this International Standard	Annex A	Annex A	Guidance on the use of this International Standard
Bibliography			Bibliography
Alphabetical index of terms			

About Authors

RAMESH C GROVER

Founder Director of India's leading Consultancy and Training Organization, Quality Growth Services Pvt Ltd (QGS), New Delhi, (Estd.1994), Ramesh C Grover is a Chemical Engineer from IIT, Delhi. Having more than 35 years of vast experience in the field of Management System Consulting, Training and Auditing. He is among the first five Registered Lead Auditor with IRCA, UK on ISO 9001, ISO 14001 and OHSAS 18001. He has assisted more than 3000 organizations in more than 20 countries including UK, Belgium, Thailand, Egypt, Sri Lanka, Bangladesh, Indonesia, Malaysia etc. for developing their Management Systems on various certifications. He is a well known faculty on various courses on Quality, Environment, Health & Safety Systems.

SACHIN GROVER

A Mechanical Engineer from PESIT, Bengaluru, Sachin Grover is the Country Head of ASR Certification Services Pvt Ltd. He is a Qualified Lead Auditor of ISO 9001, ISO 14001, ISO 27001, ISO 50001 and OHSAS 18001. Having an experience of more than 15 years in the field of Management System consultancy and Auditing. Have provided his expertise in more than 1000 organizations in more than 10 countries on various management system standards. His ideas on technological innovations have been implemented in many industries. He is a Six Sigma Black Belt and a TPM practitioner having assisted many organizations in implementing the tool. He has been the guest faculty at Amity University (on behalf of BSI) for providing Six Sigma trainings to many batches of MBA's.

This Book Contains Expert Advice on How to Prepare for ISO 45001:2018, Implementation and Auditing

This book gives *Guidance on the Implementation and auditing of ISO 45001:2018 in a simple form.* The book has been published with the aim to give you the knowledge and practical advice on preparing for ISO 45001:2018 implementations without much stress, or struggle. The book will also help the auditors, for Internal as well as External audits, in *"What to Look for"* during the Audit.

The book will help you to learn:

- Understanding the ISO 45001:2018 clauses and the benefits of its implementation
- Strategizing for ISO 45001:2018 implementation
- What the organizations should do to implement it
- What the Auditors need to look for during audit of ISO 45001:2008

The book contains examples of how an organization interprets and establishes the system for easy implementation of Occupational Health & Safety (OH&S) Management systems in the organisation

I find the book very informative, guiding the industry in a very systematic way to implement ISO 45001:2018. The authors have put in their knowledge and rich experience.

The book written by Mr. Ramesh C Grover and Mr. Sachin Grover provides a step by step practical guidance that will help putting in place an Occupational Health & Safety management system specially focused on ISO 45001:2018. I am confident that the book will be useful for all types of industries in controlling their OH&S issues and of great use to Internal Auditors as well as External Auditors in not only verifying the compliance to the standard requirements but continually improving the systems.

RAJIV PABI
Ex. President (Marketing)
INDIA GLYCOLS LIMITED,
Noida, Uttar Pradesh,
India

www.ingramcontent.com/pod-product-compliance
Lightning Source LLC
Chambersburg PA
CBHW030927180526
45163CB00002B/484